Artemis

Virgin Goddess of the Sun & Moon

Sorita D'Este

Published by Avalonia

BM Avalonia
London
WC1N 3XX
England, UK

www.avaloniabooks.co.uk

First Edition August 2005
Copyright © Sorita D'Este

Design by Avalonia
Illustrations by Brian Andrews © 2005

ISBN 1-905297-02-5

Artemis

Virgin Goddess of the Sun & Moon

Sorita D'Este

Hail to thee, Maiden blest,
Proudest and holiest:
God's Daughter, great in bliss, Leto-born, Artemis!
Hail to thee, Maiden, fair
Fairest of all that are.

Hippolytus, Euripides
(trans. Gilbert Murray)

Dedication

This book is dedicated to *Merlyn & Epona* of the *Children of Artemis*. Their work and commitment to the mysteries have, more than any other, led to a renewed interest in the *Lady of the Beasts* who roams the wild mountains and woodlands. Blessed Be.

Table of Contents

Author's Foreword

Artemis, the ancient Greek goddess of the hunt and virginity has captured the imagination of many people throughout the ages. Poets have written about Artemis as the ultimate unobtainable prize, artists have portrayed her surrounded by her hunting dogs, wild animals and of course with her bow and quiver of arrows always ready for the kill. For thousands of years, pilgrims have visited her temples and sanctuaries to ask for her help in matters of childbirth, healing and devotion, and today tourists still marvel at the unique beauty and mystery of her famous temple at Ephesus.

I personally first encountered the goddess Artemis in a poem by the American poet, Edmund Clarence Stedman (1833 – 1908) entitled "*Orion: An Epic Poem*":

> *Of Artemis,—her bow, with points drawn back,*
> *A golden hue on her white rounded breast*
> *Reflecting, while the arrow's ample barb*
> *Gleams o'er her hand, and at his heart is aim'd.*

This book is the result of research and work which I started in 2000, when I, with fervor, started a research project on the Greek goddess Hekate. My research took me down various avenues and time after time, Artemis was waiting, in one form or another at the end of them.

I realised that there were no books exclusively dedicated to the stories, myths and powers of this Olympian goddess. Having mentioned it to a few friends along the way, I had no choice but to finish it. In this I have to express my gratitude to my partner, David Rankine, for his support and help with some of the research and to Merlyn and Epona of the Children of Artemis, for their constant reminders and for the enthusiasm they have shown.

In this book I have endeavoured to present a more holistic portrayal of Artemis than the simplistic image of her as the virgin huntress of the moon that has been popularized over the last century. As you read through the chapters, which tell her stories and draw on over a millennia of classical sources, you will discover a more complex and detailed perception of Artemis.

You will find that Artemis had solar qualities as well as the lunar qualities for which she is now best known. Though a virgin she was the goddess who presided over childbirth. Artemis was worshipped by warriors for her martial qualities, and had a vengeful side which manifested in a wide range of punishments inflicted on people who offended her. Artemis was also a goddess of song and dance.

Researching Artemis made it clear that the classic sources when considered together present a picture of a complex goddess with many different qualities and roles. Although she does have the qualities of being a lunar goddess and virgin huntress as she is popularly portrayed, there is so much more to Artemis than this.

It is my hope that this book will provide the reader with a glimpse into the multifaceted world of this fascinating goddess.

Sorita D'Este
London, 2005

1. Who was Artemis?

To those who worshipped in her temples and sanctuaries in ancient times, Artemis was a goddess of childbirth and of initiation rites for young girls. A gentle goddess who was fiercely protective of those she cared for, especially of her mother and her virgin attendants.

The twin sister of the solar god Apollo, Artemis was the daughter of the Titan goddess Leto and of the king of the Olympian gods, Zeus. She played a significant role in many of the myths of Ancient Greece and her temple at Ephesus was considered to be one of the Seven Wonders of the Ancient World.[1]

Whilst we cannot say for certain where and when exactly Artemis' worship originated, we know that both Artemis and her twin brother Apollo were already well known during the Mycenaean era, as votive offerings to both have been found dating back to around 1300 BCE.

The Mycenaeans were fierce and effective warriors who were also excellent engineers. Most historians believe that the Mycenaean civilization arose from the earlier Minoan culture, which supports the theory that Artemis may have originally been the goddess now known as the *Minoan Lady of the Beasts*.

Temples and sanctuaries to Artemis existed throughout the Greek world and stretched into Anatolia[2] and Greek colonies as far afield as Sicily and Gaul[3].

Although the exact meaning of the name *Artemis* is not known for certain, the Roman writer Strabo suggested a meaning for it in his writings, saying that she made people *'Artemeas'* which means *Safe and Sound.*[4]

---

[1] Alongside the Great Pyramid of Giza, The Hanging Gardens of Babylon, The Colossus of Rhodes, The Statue of Zeus at Olympia, The Mausoleum at Halicarnassus and the Lighthouse of Alexandria.
[2] The area known today asTurkey.
[3] Modern day France
[4] *Strabo 14.1.6.*

Plato suggested that Artemis took her name from her healthy (*artemes*) and well-ordered nature, and possibly due to her disliking sexual intercourse (*ton aroton misesasa*).[5]

Artemis was always described as being very tall and beautiful, overshadowing her companion nymphs. She was frequently depicted with animal companions, as would be expected for a hunting goddess and mistress of the animals.

> "*With head and forehead Artemis overtops the rest (of her companion Nymphs), and though all are lovely, there is no mistaking which is she.*"[6]

Many of the earlier representations of Artemis show her as a winged goddess, such as the image depicted on the Francois Vase and on a gold necklace found on Rhodes. In both these images she is shown as *Potnia Theron*, the *Lady of the Beasts*. On the vase she is shown holding a large feline in her right hand and a stag in the left. The necklace shows her holding two large felines, which may be either lions or leopards. Winged depictions of goddesses are unusual amongst the Greek gods, although not unique. The goddesses Nike (goddess of victory) and Nemesis (goddess of vengeance) are both depicted as winged.

The depiction of Artemis famously associated with Ephesus is one of the most unusual. Although nothing is left of the original, smaller replicas survived showing the goddess standing upright adorned with the images of many wild animals on both her body and headdress. This depiction shows Artemis with what seem to be numerous breasts, hinting at her origins in an earlier mother goddess cult. It has been suggested that the statue depicts eggs, rather than breasts on the body. Both breasts and eggs have strong associations with fertility.

---

[5] *Plato, Cratylus.*
[6] *Odyssey 6.102.*

Artemis the Huntress
Based on the statue known as Artemis of Versailles, this image shows the goddess reaching for an arrow in her quiver whilst holding a stag by its antlers.

The statue further depicts bees on the robe of the goddess, recalling the title of *Melissae*, or *bees*, which was used for her priestesses. The headdress that she is shown with on some of these statues was a turret crown, originally associated with the goddess Cybele. Cybele's cult and worship was subsumed by Artemis and it is likely that the image that we know as *Artemis of Ephesus* was originally a depiction of Cybele, who was a mother goddess with strong associations with fertility.

As the huntress Artemis was most often portrayed with her bow and quiver of arrows, which had been given to her as a young girl by the Cyclops, the one-eyed giants who specialized in making weapons, at the behest of Zeus. The most popular modern portrayals of Artemis are based on images such as the sculpture known as *Artemis of Versailles*, which is currently on display in the Louvre, Paris. This is one of many Roman statues which are believed to be copies of an earlier Greek depiction of the goddess. Artemis is shown with her quiver of arrows, usually in a running position with a stag, deer or dog at her side reaching for an arrow in her quiver.

This image of Artemis as the hunter is the one which inspired later artists, such as Renoir and an unknown artist from the School of Fountainebleu who both created beautiful paintings of the goddess.

Artemis is also described in the *Illiad*, where her beauty and height are both emphasised,[7] which is further supported by Homer in the *Odyssey* when he comments that even amongst the most beautiful maidens Artemis was conspicuous.[8] Euripides described Artemis as the *"fairest of all that are"*.[9]

Ovid described her in his *Metamorphoses* saying that she stood a head taller than her attendant nymphs.[10] The Titan goddess Aura, when she was a companion to Artemis, commented on the roundness of Artemis' breasts, and on her soft arms, saying with her beauty and figure she could also be a goddess of marriage.[11]

---

[7] *Illiad 6.93.109.*
[8] *Odyssey 6.102-9.*
[9] *Euripides, Hippolytus.*
[10] *Ovid, Metamorphoses 3.138.*
[11] *Nonnus, Dionysiaca 48.360.*

2. The Birth of the Divine Twins

Artemis was the older twin sister of the sun god Apollo. They were born of a union between the Titan goddess Leto and the Olympian Zeus, king of the gods. Zeus, who was well known for his many amorous conquests, was married to the goddess of marriage, Hera, who did not approve of his love affairs. Hera was both jealous and angry at Leto's relationship with her husband and as a result forced the pregnant Leto out into the wilds to give birth to her children.

Classical writers gave varying accounts of the story of Leto's pregnancy and birth, which placed emphasis on different parts of the story. Many texts, including the writings of Apollodorus, Ovid, Pausanias, Strabo, the *Dionysiaca*, the *Greek Lyric V Scolia Frag 886*, Hesiod's *Theogony*, the *Homeric Hymns* and Pindar's *Processional Song on Delos* all gave accounts of the events that follow. The following is an overview of the story based on a combination of these accounts:

Hera, the queen of the gods was furious when she found out about Leto's pregnancy. She decided to send the Python of Delphi (a serpent or a dragon in different tales) to chase Leto across the land, harrying her and preventing her from stopping or resting anywhere to give birth. Furthermore, Hera forced the rulers of all the various lands to not give Leto sanctuary, preventing her from giving birth on land.

At one point, Leto, desperate for sanctuary, assumed the form of a wolf, and hid with a pack of wolves. This is why the wolf would later become an animal considered sacred to both Artemis and Apollo.

Leto travelled through many different places, whilst constantly being chased by the Python, and many of these places were later named in honour of the auspicious birth of the twins. Notably, Pausanias mentioned Zoster in Attica, home of a shrine to Leto, Artemis and Apollo. It was at Zoster that Leto let loose her girdle and managed to get some rest, before continuing on her journey to find a safe place to give birth to her children. The term *zoster* comes from the Greek word for *girdle* or *belt*.

Zeus, the father of the gods, who impregnated Leto, was said by some to have helped at the last hour. Zeus commanded the North Wind Boreas to bear her safely away from the Python to the island of Delos. And it was there at Delos, that Leto was finally given sanctuary, rather than turned away.

So it was that Delos became the birthplace of Artemis and Apollo. In some versions of the myth, Leto gave birth to the twins under an old palm tree, which is why the palm became sacred to both Leto and Artemis.

In the story recounted in the *Homeric Hymns*, the goddess of childbirth Eileithyia, who was at this point considered separate to Artemis, was kept occupied on Mount Olympus by Hera, to stop her from attending the birth. However the other goddesses sent the messenger goddess Iris to bring Eileithyia to aid Leto, which she did.

Although the birth of Artemis had been very easy, that of Apollo was not and he did not leave the womb until Eileithyia arrived on Delos, when his birth began, with Eileithyia assisted also by Artemis.

When Artemis and Apollo reached adulthood, Apollo took revenge on the Python for its treatment of his mother by killing it. In some versions of the myths Artemis helped him. Once this was done, Apollo usurped the shrine of the Python at Delphi thus becoming the God of the Delphic Oracle. The divine twins went on to eliminate an assortment of rulers who had turned their pregnant mother away when she was looking for sanctuary.

In Pausanias an alternative parentage is given for Artemis, suggesting that her mother is the earth goddess Demeter, rather than Leto.

> *"That Artemis was the daughter, not of Leto but of Demeter, which is the Egyptian account, the Greeks learned from Aiskhylos the son of Euphorion."*[12]

In some versions of the story of Artemis' birth, Ortygia is named as her place of birth. Ortygia is however also an older name for Delos. According to the legends Delos sprang from the sea when Asteria, the

---

[12] *Pausanias 8.37.3.*

sister of Leto, flung herself into the sea to escape the advances of Zeus, who transformed her into a giant quail.

Delos was believed to have once been a floating island, which may provide another reason as to why Leto gave birth there. Hera forbade Leto from giving birth on solid earth (terra firma) and if Delos was a floating island at the time, it would explain why Leto could give birth there safely.

In alternative versions of the story, Zeus changed Leto into a quail to help her reach Delos and fastened the floating island with adamantine (a term used for diamonds and meaning *"unconquerable"*) chains to the bottom of the ocean so that it would be a safe resting place for her to give birth.

The name Ortygia is also later given to Apollo's oxen and is a name which was associated with *ortux,* a type of quail, by the ancient Greeks.

A grove near Ephesus was also named Ortygia and the Ephesians believed, or pretended to believe, that Artemis and Apollo were born there.

In honour of the birth of Artemis and Apollo, the festival of First Fruits or *Thargelia* was celebrated on the 6th and 7th day of the month of Thargelion. The 6th day of every month was also considered sacred to Artemis.

3. Temples & Sanctuaries of Artemis

Temples and sanctuaries honouring Artemis permeated the Greek world. In addition to archeological evidence, clues to the location of some of Artemis' sacred places can be found in plays, comedies, poetry and in many other literary works from the ancient world. Pausanias, in his classic work *Guide to Greece*, a second century CE travel guide to the Greek world, lists a large number of temples and shrines of Artemis. We can also determine the location of some temples and shrines through titles given to Artemis. These titles are listed with other cult titles in chapter 6 *Titles of Artemis*.

Many of Artemis' temples were built near to springs and rivers, this may have been for practical reasons, but there is some evidence that suggests that these were considered sacred by worshippers, as votive offerings have been found in the water at many sites.

Statues often played an important part in the worship of Artemis. There are accounts of devotional rites in honour of Artemis which were held around statues, and legends which show the great importance which was placed upon specific cult statues. An example of this is the rites held at Sparta to *Artemis Orthia* where young men were ritually scourged, whilst a priestess bearing the wooden cult statue of Artemis looked on. In another early account young virgin girls and boys carried a statue of *Artemis Ephesia* out to a field near the sea, where they dance and sing around it, making offerings of salt.[13]

The best known of Artemis' temples are those at Ephesus and Brauron, which I will consider in more detail in the following sections. Ephesus is one of the largest known temples to any goddess and is considered to be one of the Seven Wonders of the Ancient World. At the temple of Artemis at Brauron, young girls were dedicated to the virgin goddess, and women would make pilgrimages to Brauron where they made offerings to Artemis for help in childbirth.

---

[13] *Etymologicum Magnum.*

Artemis of Brauron

The temple of *Artemis Brauronia* stood on what Euripides may have been referring to as the "holy stairs of Brauron" in his play, *Iphigeneia in Tauris* and was sometimes called the *The Parthenon of the Bear Maidens,* referring to one of its most famous rites. It is believed to have been one of the twelve ancient cities of Attica, which eventually became unified with Athens.

Votive offerings dating to the 9th and 8th century BCE have been found at the site and it is suggested that early worship of the goddess at Brauron was focused on the sacred spring and cave which became part of the temple complex. Archaeological evidence indicates that the site itself had been occupied previously from as early as the Neolithic period through to the late Bronze Age.

The stone temple on the site was built around the 6th century BCE by the Athenian ruler Peisistratos, or possibly by his sons. Peisistratos also established an additional sanctuary to *Artemis Brauronia* in the Acropolis. He incorporated many Brauronian rites into Athenian public life, further emphasising the importance of the temple at Brauron as a result and increasing the importance of Artemis in Athens. The remains of the stoa to *Artemis Brauronia* can still be found amongst the ruins of the Acropolis today.

An official site inspection list from the 3rd century BCE provides evidence that the site included a temple, a Parthenon, stables, a wrestling school and a gymnasium. The temple was flooded later in the 3rd century BCE by the river Eurasinos and was not rebuilt. Nine centuries later a Christian basilica to St George was built near the sacred well.

Some believed that the temple at Brauron was established by Iphigeneia. According to various accounts, King Agamemnon, the father of Iphigeneia, was murdered by his wife. Orestes, the brother of Iphigeneia, took revenge for the death of his father by killing his mother. In an effort to make amends with the gods for this act, he was told by an Oracle to steal the cult statue of Artemis from the Scythians in Tauris.

What Orestes did not know was that his sister Iphigeneia had been taken to Tauris by Artemis. He was caught and brought before his sister to be sacrificed to the goddess. Iphigeneia upon recognising her brother helped him escape and together they stole the statue as they fled.

Pausanias wrote of a legend in which Iphigeneia left the wooden image of *Artemis Tauropolos* at Brauron when she and Orestes fled from the Taureans.[14] In another passage he wrote that he believed the statue was instated at Limnaion, where Orestes was king and the goddess was worshipped as *Artemis Orthia*.[15] He also referred to the sanctuary of *Artemis Brauronia* at the Acropolis,[16] from which the Persian king Xerxes stole the image of *Artemis Brauronia* from the sanctuary when he attacked Athens.[17]

At the temple in Brauron, Artemis' followers worshipped her as a goddess of protection during childbirth and of female children until puberty. Women who travelled from afar to make offerings to Artemis at Brauron for protection during childbirth would dedicate prized possessions to the goddess as well as a set of clothing upon successful birth. Gems, mirrors and rings have been recovered from the spring and the stream at Brauron, which shows the importance that was placed on the help Artemis could give in this matter. Interestingly, the clothes of women who died in childbirth were offered to Iphigeneia, at a shrine which was near the main temple at Brauron.

The Brauronia festival was held every four years at the temple, unsurprisingly it was a festival which was held largely for women. Much of what is known of this ceremony comes from images depicted on the remains of pottery fragments and vessels which have been found in and around the sanctuary. Additionally, Aristophanes, the comic playwright, also provides us with some useful passages concerning activities at this temple.[18]

Many of the images found depict young girls, sometimes naked and in other instances shown wearing chitons (hunting tunics). They are

---

[14] *Pausanias 1.33.1.*
[15] *Pausanias 3.16.7.*
[16] *Pausanias 1.23.7.*
[17] *Pausanias 8.46.3.*
[18] *Peace 872-6 and Lysistrata 638f.*

shown dancing or running near an altar, sometimes bearing torches, sometimes twigs or crowns of leaves. Additionally they are at times depicted in saffron coloured robes known as *Krokotoi*.

There are differing opinions regarding the age range of the girls who went to Brauron. Some writers suggest that they were around five to ten years old,[19] others suggest that girls went there during puberty, after which they would be ready to marry and be dedicated to the goddesses Hera and Aphrodite. In the *Lysistrata* a woman recounts how at the age of ten years old she took the role of the she-bear at Brauron.[20]

Some images show a fire burning on the altar. Some fragments show the twigs being used to sprinkle water from chalices, implying ritual lustration. It is also believed that a goat was sacrificed to the goddess as part of the ceremony.

During the festival, young girls participated in the ceremonies as *Arktoi*, which means *she-bear*. This custom has its origins in a story which tells of the killing of a tame she-bear who frequented the sanctuary.

A young girl teased the she-bear, which became agitated. It attacked the girl and ripped out her eye. Subsequently the girl's brothers took revenge on the bear, killing it. Artemis retaliated and sent a plague to the sanctuary. In desperation the people of Brauron consulted an Oracle and were told that the only way to appease the goddess was for the girls to take the role of the she-bear in a mystery play.

It may have been that the she-bear which was killed was previously involved in some of the festivities at Brauron, alternatively this may have been a completely new addition to the rituals to honour the bear which was killed. Either way, it was said that all Athenian girls had to dance the she-bear at Brauron prior to marriage. In reality it would have only been possible for a priviledged few.

The act of dancing the she-bear prior to marriage could also be seen as representing an initiatory experience, marking the transition from

---

[19] *Suidas, Arktos e Brauroniois.*
[20] *Aristophanes, Lysistrata 638.*

childhood to womanhood. The dance itself could be seen as representing the transformation of the girls, from the wild and untamed status of childhood to that of a respectable life as a married woman.

Newly wed girls would dedicate their virginal robes to Artemis as an offering, thanking the goddess for protecting their virginity[21]. Upon marriage they rededicated themselves to Hera, as the goddess of marriage and Aphrodite, the goddess of sensual love.

Although Brauron was primarily a temple for women, statues and other depictions of young boys have also been found on the site. Some modern writers have speculated that it is possible that boys were allowed at the temple, providing that they were part of a girl-boy twin, honouring the divine twins, Artemis and Apollo.

Artemis of Ephesus

The temple of Artemis at Ephesus was and remains the most famous temple to Artemis and indeed any of the ancient goddesses. It was written about and visited by people from all over the ancient world, and continues to be a popular attraction for modern day tourists who wander through the ruins with the hope of glimpsing its former glory.

Artemis was celebrated at this temple with the title of *Artemis Ephesia* which simply means *Artemis of Ephesus*. Hyginus wrote that the temple of Artemis at Ephesus was one of the Seven Wonders of the Ancient World.[22]

The site had long been used for religious ceremonies and historians have suggested several goddesses as being the original goddess of Ephesus before they were subsumed in the worship of Artemis. Notably these include the Anatolian goddess Hannahanna, and the Asian goddesses Anahita and Cybele. Earlier depictions of Artemis hint at these older goddesses.

The rites and festivals of Artemis which were celebrated at Ephesus, spread throughout the ancient world. Pausanias mentions an image

---

[21] *Suidas, Lysizonos gune.*
[22] *Hyginus, Fabulae 223, circa 2nd century CE.*

of *Artemis Ephesia* in the government offices of Megalopolis[23], a statue of *Artemis Ephesia* in the market-place of Corinthos[24] and a sanctuary to *Artemis Ephesia* in the village of Alea in Arcadia.[25]

Strabo refers to a temple of *Artemis Ephesia* at Massilia (Marseilles) in Gaul[26] (France) and also that the Iberians (modern Spain) practised the sacred rites of *Artemis Ephesia*.[27] The temple at Massilia included a reproduction of the cult statue of Ephesus, after Artemis appeared to the noblewoman Aristarkha in a dream and instructed her to take a copy of the statue with her to Massilia. In acknowledgement of this she was subsequently appointed the priestess of Artemis at Massilia.[28]

The importance of Ephesus is further stressed by Strabo when he mentions that this was the only Ionian temple which was not burned down and destroyed by the Persian King Xerxes when he invaded the area.[29]

The temple of Artemis at Ephesus is believed to be built on the site of an earlier goddess shrine, dating back to as early as 1000 BCE. The shrine would have been on a marshy strip of land near the river Selinus. The first temple on the site was built around 550 BCE, paid for by the Lydian King Croesus and designed by the architect Chersiphon. The temple was destroyed and rebuild several times in its history. Strabo wrote that it was built and destroyed seven times, and although evidence to support this statement is lacking, archeologists have found evidence that the temple on the site was rebuilt at least four times.

Most famously the temple was burned to the ground in 356 BCE, on the night of the birth of Alexander the Great[30]. Eastern soothsayers who visited the ruins of the temple prophesied that the day that the temple burned down was an omen predicting that a great force which

---

[23] *Pausanias 8.30.6.*
[24] *Pausanias 2.2.6.*
[25] *Pausanias 8.23.1*, see also *7.22.6* and *10.26.6.*
[26] *Strabo 4.1.8.*
[27] *Strabo 4.1.5.*
[28] *Strabo 4.1.4.*
[29] *Strabo 14.1.5.*
[30] Some historians have dates this to 21st July 356 BCE

would destroy Asia came into the world. They were correct as this force proved to be Alexander himself. It was a man named Herostratus who destroyed the temple in an attempt to immortalize his name. This he certainly succeeded in doing. Plutarch wrote of this incident saying that Artemis was too busy taking care of the birth of Alexander to send help to her threatened temple.

In 334 BCE, after he conquered Asia Minor, Alexander offered to rebuild the temple, but the Ephesians refused his offer of help. They told him that a god could not build a temple to another god, emphasising the widespread belief that, as the most powerful man in the ancient world at the time, Alexander himself was a god incarnate. The temple was eventually restored years later in 323 BCE.

The historian Herodotus told of the founding of the city around 1000 BCE through the advice of the Delphic Oracle of Apollo. Androklos, the son of King Kodors of Athens, went to Anatolia, having been told "*a fish and a boar will show you the place*".

Whilst his men prepared a fire to cook a fish they had caught, nearby bushes caught flame, scaring a boar which had been hiding in them. Androklos pursued the boar and killed it. He subsequently remembered the words of the Oracle and built the city of Ephesus where the boar had been killed. This can also be seen as a sacrificial offering for the foundation of the city which would be sacred to Artemis, goddess of the hunt. It may also be noted that the boar and fish are both sacred to Artemis.

The early text of the *Etymologicum Magnum* details an interesting story that gives the origins of practices that occurred at Ephesus. It recounts the story of princess Clymena, who with a number of boys and young virgins carried a statue of Artemis out of the city. They set it up in a field near the sea and danced and sang around it. They wanted to offer food to the goddess, but had only salt to give. The next year the ceremony was not repeated, and the young participants were punished by an epidemic sent by Artemis. Subsequently meals were regularly offered to Artemis to propitiate her.[31]

---

[31] *Etymologicum Magnum, 252.11.*

Pausanias waxed lyrical about *Artemis Ephesia*, writing *"All cities worship Artemis Ephesia"*.[32] He wrote that she was universally held in very high renown due to the antiquity and size of her temple. He further said that her importance was due to the fame of the Amazons who he believed dedicated the cult image and founded the city of Ephesus itself.

Artemis also has the distinction of being referred to in the New Testament of *The Bible*. When Paul visited Ephesus the people cried *Great is Artemis of Ephesus"*, emphasising their support for their goddess.[33]

---

[32] *Pausanias 4.31.7.*
[33] *Acts 19.*

Artemis of Ephesus
This image depicts Artemis Ephesia and is based on surviving copies of the cult statue that once stood in her temple in Ephesus.

Temples of Artemis by Region

From ancient records we know of temples and sanctuaries throughout the ancient Greek world. These are listed below, though there may well have been others that were destroyed or for which records have not survived.

Central Greece
Central Greece was divided into a number of regions, and amongst these regions many temples to Artemis were found. We know temples were located at Amarynthos, Amphissa, Antikyra, Artemision, Aulis, Boulis, Calydon, Delphi, Hyampolis, Kirrha, Kyrtones, Lilaia, Naupaktos, Oiantheia, Plataia, Tanagra and Thebes.

Southern Greece
By far the largest number of temples and groves dedicated to her were located in southern Greece. There were also temples on the islands of Aigina and Salamis off the southern Greek coast. Temples and groves of Artemis existed at Aigeira, Aigion, Akakesion, Alagonia, Alea, Amyklai, Argos, Athens, Athmonia, the Azanian Hills, Boiai, Brauron, Corinthos, Dereion, Eleusis, Elis, Epidauros, Epidauros Limera, Helos, Hermione, Hypsous, Kaphya, Karyai, Korone, Letrinoi, Limnai, Lousoi, Lykoa, Marios, Megalopolis, Megara, Messene, Mothone, Mount Artemisios, Mount Koryphon, Mount Krathis, Mount Lykone, Mounykhia, Myrrhinos, Olympia, Oresthasion, Orkhomenos, Orneai, Pagai, Patrai, Pellene, Phelloi, Pheneos, Phigalia, Phlya, Pisa, Pyrrhikhos, Sikyon, Skias, Skillos, Sparta (including a shrine on the road to Arcadia), Stymphalos, Tegea, Teuthis, Teuthrone, Trikolonoi, Troizenos, Zoitea and Zoster.

Northern Greece
There are only two references to Artemis temples in northern Greece, which were at Melite, and Pherai in Thessalia.

The Aegean Sea
Many of the islands in the Aegean Sea had temples to Artemis on them. These include Delos in the Cyclades Islands (famous as the place of her birth), the Hekatonnesoi Islands, Ikaria, Samos, Rhodes and Crete.

Turkey

There were also many temples to Artemis in what is now Turkey, as the famous temple at Ephesus produced a wide range of worship. The large number of towns and villages with sacred shrines or temples to Artemis in Turkey included Adrasteia, Astyra, Bargylia, Bubastos, Byzantion, Ephesus, Hypoplakinan Thebes, Kalydna, Kastabos, Korakios, Lake Gygaia, Magnesia, Miletos, Mount Sipylos, Ortygia, Perge, Phrygia, Pitane, Pygela and Pylai.

Greek Colonies

When the Greeks traveled and traded, they took their deities with them. As a result of this there were also temples around the Mediterranean and up into Scythia (modern Ukraine). Artemis temples at Greek colonies were found at Khersonesos in Scythia, Iberia (modern Spain), Massilia (Marseilles) in Southern Gaul (modern France), Capua and the Henetoi regions of Italy, and Syrakouse in Sikelia (modern Sicily).

4. Festivals of Artemis

The ancient Greeks loved their deities and they often celebrated them through elaborate festivals. We know that many temples held festivals with a local theme, and that festivals and religious rites were also held at many of the smaller shrines and santuaries. What we cannot say for certain is when exactly each of these took place.

The ancient Greeks did not have one universally accepted calendar, instead each state had their own, based around a lunisolar calendar, taking into account, as the name suggests, both solar and lunar cycles. This makes it near to impossible to attribute festival dates in the various ancient calendars to modern dates in the Gregorian calendar accurately.

The Attic calendar, which was used in Athens, had two months in Spring which were named after *Artemis Elaphebolos* and *Artemis Mounykhia*. This accentuates the importance of the Artemis festivals which were celebrated in the region during this time. The Attic calendar consisted of the months Hekatombaion, Metageitnion, Boedromion, Pyanopsion, Maimakterion, Poseideon, Gamelion, Anethesterion, Elaphebolion, Mounykhion, Thargelion and Skirophorion.

In Delos, the calendar shared some names with the Attic calendar. The sequence of months there was Hekatombaion, Metageitnion, Bouphonion, Apatourion, Aresion, Poseideon, Lenaion, Hieros, Galaxion, Artemision, Thargelion and Panemos. The month of *Artemision* was named in honour of Artemis.

Festivals and rites were held at many of Artemis' temples and sanctuaries, such as the famous Brauronia festival which was held every four years in Brauron.[34] The festivals of Artemis which have been described in most detail by ancient writers are the Brauronia, Charisteria, Elaphebolia, Hiketeria, Laphria, Mounykhia and Thargelia.

---

[34] The Brauronia is discussed in more detail in *Chapter 3, Temples & Santuaries of Artemis.*

Some festivals are mentioned in passing by ancient writers like Pausanias, who probably expected their audience to be familiar with these ceremonies, resulting in us having festival names with few details.

From Pausanias we know that annual festivals were held to *Artemis Daphnaií* and *Artemis Elaphiaía* at Olympia. He mentions a festival which was held to *Artemis Hymnia* on the border of Orkhomenos in Arcadia, where priests of Artemis lived their lives in purity, abstaining from sex and washing, and never entering private homes. He also recorded that an annual festival was held to *Artemis Diktynna* at the temple in Hypsous, Lacedaimonia.

Pausanias refers to an annual festival called Saronia[35] but there is little known about the festival itself. Saronia refers to an Argosian hero, Saron, who established a sanctuary in honour of Artemis near Troizenos in Argolis, where this festival was held.[36]

A further festival is recorded by Xenophon, when he wrote of a failed attack on Thebes on the last day of a festival of *Artemis Eukleia*. The date for the event is given to be 392 BCE. Another festival is mentioned by Hesychius when he referred to female dancers from Sparta who danced at a festival for *Artemis Korythalia.*

Charisteria

Charisteria, meaning *thanksgiving,* took place on 6th Boedromion, and honoured the victory over the Persians at Marathon. It celebrated a victory which took place on a different date, although this does not seem to be recorded.

At the Charisteria five hundred goats were sacrificed to *Artemis Agrotera* and to *Ares Enyalios*. The goats were taken to the temple of *Artemis Agrotera* on the Ilissos in a ceremonial procession and then sacrificed. It is said that the Athenians originally offered a goat for

---

[35] *Pausanias 2.32.10.*
[36] *Pausanias 2.32.10.*

every Persian slain, but that so many Persians were killed that it would have wiped out the entire goat population to continue to do so.[37]

This sanctuary was unique amongst Artemis shrines in that it was to her and the war god Ares, rather than the usual association of Artemis with her brother Apollo, and may be connected to the worship of Artemis alongside Ares by the Amazons.

Elaphebolia

The festival of Elaphebolia was celebrated widely, but the town of Hyanpolis in Phocis was reknowned for their celebration of it. The festival there, held on 6th Elaphebolion, celebrated the victory of the townspeople over the Thessalians who had ravaged the countryside surrounding them.

During the festival *elaphos* cakes would be made of dough, honey and sesame seeds. The cakes, which are thought to have been made in the shape of a stag or deer, were offered to *Artemis Elaphebolos* during the festivities.

The *elaphos* cakes are also mentioned by Herodotus when he wrote about three hundred Corcyraean boys who were sent to Alyattes to be made eunuchs. When they stopped at Samos, the locals encouraged them to take sanctuary in the temple of Artemis. This angered the Corinthians who forbid the Samians from taking food into the temple, in an effort to starve the boys into submission.

The Samians, in an effort to save the boys, invented a new festival to Artemis. Each night choirs of young boys and virgin girls encircled the temple with cakes of sesame and honey in their hands, which the Corcyraean boys grabbed, eating them to stay alive. The Corinthians eventually gave up and the Samians returned the boys to their homes. Afterwards this festival continued and was said to be the original source of the Elaphebolia festival.[38]

---

[37] *Xenophon, Anabasis.*
[38] *Herodotus, The Histories, 3.48.*

Hiketeria

Plutarch in his *Life of Thesus* records that on 6th Mounykhion a procession of virgin girls would walk to the Delphinion, each carrying an olive twig bound with white wool.[39] Although there is no record of the name of this festival, it is possible it was called Hiketeria[40] after the suppliant's twigs carried by the girls (*hiketeria*). It has been suggested that these twigs served an apotropaic function, providing protection from evil.

We know that the sixth day of the month was sacred to Artemis, so it seems fairly certain that this ceremony of maiden girls was in her honour.

Laphria

The Laphria was held at Patrai and was a rather grim festival where many different animals were burned alive. This was an important state festival and the main festival days were public holidays to allow everyone to participate.

Pausanias gave a detailed description of the festival in his *Description of Hellas*. Around the altar, a circle logs of green wood was placed, with dry wood on the altar. Earth was piled on the altar steps to allow a smooth ascent to the altar.

A procession to Artemis began the festival, with the officiating priestess riding in a chariot pulled by deer, imitating the golden chariot of Artemis. The following day the main part of the festival would take place.

First the fruits of cultivated trees were placed on the altar, this was followed by animals. The animals were thrown onto the altar before it was lit, burning the fruit offerings and the live animals. There were a variety of animals recorded as being sacrificed in this manner at

---

[39] *Attische Feste* – Ludwig Deubner, 1932, p201.
[40] *Festivals of Attica* – Erica Simon, p79.

Patria, including bears, boars, deer and wolves. Any animals which tried to escape were thrown back onto the pyre.

Mounykhia

The festival of Mounykhia was celebrated on 16th Mounykhion to Artemis at Piraeus. This was a full moon ceremony and was sacred to Artemis-Hekate, as small cakes called *amphiphontes* meaning *shining on both sides*, were offered to the goddess. These cakes were also offered to Hekate at suppers which were held at the crossroads in her honour. Reference is made to *dadiai* (*little torches*) decorating the cakes, much in the style of birthday cakes with small candles on them today. Some writers have even speculated that the dadiai may provide clues to the origins of our own modern birthday cake.[41]

Athenaios wrote that amphiphontes were offered at temples of Artemis and at crossroads on the sixteenth of each month, when the sky was lit by both the sun and the moon from either side and thus became *amphiphos*.[42]

After the victory over the Persians at the sea battle of Salamis, this festival was also celebrated at Mounykhia. Even though the battle took place seven months earlier, the assistance of Artemis in the battle had been vital and the victory was celebrated at this festival to honour her appropriately.

Thargelia

This festival which was the offering of the first fruits, took place on the 6th and 7th of Thargelion and marked the birthdays of Artemis and Apollo respectively.

On the first day of the festival, two people would be chosen amongst the poor. They would be given a feast of food, after which they were

---

[41] Ludwig Deubner in *Attische Feste* and H.W. Parke in *Festivals of the Athenians*, 1977.
[42] *Athenaios, Deipnosophistai 14.645a.*

beaten in an act of sympathetic magic, symbolising the purification of the city.

The next day, offerings of the first fruits, or *thargelos*, were made to the gods. The ritual offerings were followed by a hymn singing contests in which the men and boys participated.

5. The Role of Artemis in the Myths

Artemis was undoubtedly one of the most significant of the ancient Greek deities, and this is reflected by the frequency of her appearances in myths, literature and art, and the huge number of temples and shrines to her. In the myths different qualities of the character of Artemis were clearly displayed.

The following section recounts the roles she played in some of the ancient myths, indicating some of her strengths and weaknesses. These myths also give an indication of the deities whom Artemis was most associated with, such as Dionysus, Apollo and Leto.

The Aloadai Giants

The Aloadai giants were young twins described as being fifty-four feet high and eighteen feet across. At the age of nine they decided to fight the Olympian gods. They had already demonstrated their strength by capturing the war god Ares and chaining him in a brazen cauldron for thirteen months. Hermes rescued him when Eriboia, the stepmother of the giants, told him where Ares was located.[43]

To attack the Olympian gods the mighty young giants placed Mount Ossa on top of Mount Olympus, and then placed Mount Pelion on top of Mount Ossa, to create a tower to the sky to reach the gods.

The first Olympians they encountered on their raid were the goddesses Artemis and Hera. The first twin, Ephialtes, tried to force his unwanted attentions on Hera, and the second Otos did likewise to Artemis. Artemis escaped from Otos by shape-shifting into a deer, distracting the young giants. Ephialtes and Otos decided they wanted to kill this divine deer.

Artemis cunningly ran between them, and as they tried to spear her she moved too swiftly for the cumbersome giants to hit her. As a result they missed and killed each other instead, just as Artemis had

---

[43] *Illiad 5.385.*

planned.[44] The giants died at Naxos, the place where Dionysus would subsequently meet Ariadne after her abandonment by the hero Theseus.

The Hyperboreoi

Artemis was the patron deity of the mythical Hyperboreoi with her brother Apollo. The Hyperboreoi were said to be a race of long-lived men, living in a realm of eternal spring in the far north. They are mentioned in connection with Medea, who refers to them when speaking to King Pelias of Iolkos, in Thessalia.

Medea caused dragons to appear in the sky over Thessalia by using hallucinogenic drugs, and declared that they had brought the goddess with her from Hyperborea to visit his land.[45]

Artemis seems to have favoured the Hyperboreans, as she made a number of them temple attendants. She immortalized the three maidens Hekaerge, Loxo and Oupis to be attendants of the shrine on Delos.

The virgins Arge and Opis, who were attendants at the temple of Artemis on Delos were also said to come from Hyperborea.[46] In one version of the Orion tale, Artemis shot him for trying to force his attentions onto Opis.[47]

The Indian Wars of Dionysus

The *Dionysiaca* describes a conflict known as the Indian Wars of Dionysus. In this story, some of the Greek Gods were fighting each other in India, one side led by Dionysus, the beautiful god of wine and wildness and the other side by Hera, queen of the gods.

---

[44] *Apollodorus, The Library 1.53.*
[45] *Diodorus Siculus 4.50.6.*
[46] *Herodotus 4.35.1.*
[47] *Apollodorus 1.27.*

During this conflict Artemis fought on the side of Dionysus. In this tale, Artemis' friendship with Dionysus is emphasised, as well as her continued rivalry with Hera. When Hera and Artemis met in combat, Hera took advantage of her position as the wife of Zeus.

As Artemis was shooting her arrows at Hera, Hera seized one of Zeus' clouds and used it as a shield, absorbing all of the arrows. Artemis eventually ran out of arrows, at which point Hera picked a large chunk of hail out of the air, threw it at Artemis and in the process broke her bow. Hera threw a second chunk of hail at Artemis, hitting her on the chest and knocking her over.[48]

Artemis also tried to save Dionysus when he was driven mad by one of the Furies at Hera's command. Again, Hera managed to triumph over Artemis, this time by throwing a burning torch at her, driving her away and preventing her from helping Dionysus, though she did prevent wild beasts from harming the delirious god.[49]

The Sacrifice of Iphigeneia

The story of Iphigeneia tells of a young girl who became a mortal attendant of Artemis, who later made her immortal. It is believed that she could be an earlier goddess associated with childbirth, as her name has been suggested to mean *she who is born with force*. Although she is given to be the daughter of King Agamemnon, later sources, such as Antoninus Liberalis[50] claimed that she was the daughter of Perseus and Helen.

The story, which played an important role in the Trojan War was written about by many of the Greek and later Roman writers.

King Agamemnon offended Artemis by declaring that he was the greatest of hunters after killing a deer. This angered Artemis, who prevented his fleet from sailing by causing the wind to still. Agamemnon was subsequently informed by the soothsayer Kalkhas

---

[48] *Dionysiaca 36.28.*
[49] *Dionysiaca 32.100-118.*
[50] *Antoninus Liberalis, Metamorphoses, 27.*

that Artemis would not allow him to sail until he offered his most beautiful daughter Iphigeneia as a sacrifice to Artemis to appease her.

In Aeschylus' *Agamemnon* the goddess is said to have demanded the sacrifice of Iphigeneia because she was angry that a pregnant hare was killed by an eagle near the palace of Agamemnon. This was also said to be an omen for the destruction of Troy, with the hare representing Troy and the eagle the avenging Greeks.

Agamemnon placed Iphigeneia on the altar, but at the last moment Artemis replaced the girl with a deer, taking her to safety and installing her as one of her priestesses, and according to an account by Apollodorus, some claimed that Artemis also made her immortal.[51]

In the version told by Ovid in his *Metamorphoses*, Iphigeneia gave herself as a willing sacrifice, laying herself on the altar. The Priests and Agamemnon, all wept at the thought of losing her. Artemis was pleased by the girl's courage, and brought a mist over the proceedingsand in the turmoil of the ritual took Iphigeneia and left a hind in her place.

When the same story is recounted by Antoninus Liberalis, Artemis placed a bull on the altar, carrying Iphigeneia to the Sea of Pontos, naming a tribe she found there Taureans, after the bull which was sacrificed in her place.[52] Following on from this we then see the roots of the founding of the Artemis shrine at Brauron when Iphigeneia and her brother Orestes took the cult statue of Artemis from Tauros to Brauron.

Iphigeneia was sometimes also subsumed into the figure of the goddess Hekate.

> "Hesiod in the Catalogues of Women represented that
> Iphigeneia was not killed but, by the will of Artemis, became
> Hekate."[53]

---

[51] *Apollodorus E3.21.*
[52] *Antoninus Liberalis, Metamorphoses, 27.*
[53] *Catalogues of Women Frag 71 (from Pausanias 1.43.1).*

Callisto's Fall

Callisto (or Kallisto) was a princess of Lycaon, in Arcadia. She loved hunting and joined Artemis as a companion, swearing to be virginal forever and eternally loyal to Artemis. However when Zeus saw Callisto he desired her and forced himself on her, making her pregnant. In some versions of the tale he assumed the form of Artemis to get close to Callisto before molesting her.[54]

The pregnant Callisto tried to hide her pregnancy from Artemis. She managed to do so for a while, but when Artemis and her companions were bathing, the goddess realised Callisto's situation and became furious with her. According to Hesiod, Artemis in her fury turned the girl into a bear and then proceeded to hunt and kill her.[55]

Apollodorus recounts a slightly different version of the story, in which Zeus changed Callisto into a bear to protect her from Artemis and Hera. Hera however persuaded Artemis to shoot Callisto in her bear form. Apollodorus also mentioned that some claimed Artemis killed Callisto for failing to preserve her virginity. As Callisto died, Zeus took the unborn baby and gave it to Maia to rear in Arcadia, calling it Arkas, or *bear*.[56]

Both versions tell us that Zeus, mourning the death of Callisto, placed her amongst the stars, naming the constellation Arktos which means *bear*. Arktos is the constellation now known as *Ursa Major* which means *Big Bear*.

King Lygdamis of Scythia

It should already be clear that it was never wise to offend Artemis, so many thought King Lygdamis of Scythia must have been mad when he threatened that he would take his army and lay waste to the shrine of Artemis at Ephesus.

---

[54] E.g. in the *Dionysiaca*.
[55] *Hesiod, The Astronomy Frag 3 (from Pseudo-Eratosthenes, Catasterismi Frag 1.2).*
[56] *Apollodorus 3.100.*

Artemis protected her shrine by demonstrating her ability to strike from afar with her arrows of disease and protect what was dear to her. So before King Lygdamis and his army even reached Ephesus, the goddess struck them down with a terrible plague, killing them all.[57]

Queen Niobe of Thebes

Queen Niobe of Thebes, daughter of king Tantalus, was a proud woman who did not pay due respect to the gods. She had seven sons and seven daughers by her husband Amphion who all grew up to be beautiful young men and women.

One day at a ceremony in honour of the goddess Leto, Queen Niobe was heard boasting that she was more blessed than Leto, who only had one son and one daughter. Leto on hearing this insult became furious.

In her rage Leto instructed Artemis and Apollo to slay all the daughters and sons of Niobe. Using their bows, Artemis slew the daughters, whilst Apollo killed Niobe's sons. They spared only the one daughter, Khloris, and one son, Amyklas, who had prayed to Leto for forgiveness.[58]

Pausanias tells us that Khloris was originally called Meliboia, but that due to the fright of seeing her siblings killed she became extremely pale and remained that way, thereby gaining the name Khloris meaning *pale one*.

At the temple described by Pausanias at Argos, he stated that there was a statue of Khloris alongside that of Artemis. It is further interesting to note that Pausanias did not believe that any of Niobe's children survived, although he does recount the story nonetheless.[59]

Homer, who recounts the story in the *Illiad*, wrote that Niobe's children lay unburied for nine days as Zeus turned the people to stone. On the

---

[57] *Callimachus, Hymn 3 to Artemis.*
[58] *Diodorus Siculus 4.74.3., Pausanias 2.21.9.*
[59] *Pausanias 2.21.9.*

tenth day the gods took pity, returned the people to their normal state and allowed the children to be buried in tombs.

When Amphion realised that his children had been slain, he committed suicide, or according to some versions of the myth, he was also killed by Apollo when he tried to avenge the death of his children. Pausanias writes that Amphion was further punished after his death by Hades, the god of the underworld, for mocking Leto.[60]

Niobe, grieving the loss of her children, fled to Mount Sipylos in Asia Minor where she turned into a weeping rock. The endless tears from the rock formed a stream, the Achelous. In the *Dionysiaca* it is suggested that it might be Nemesis, the goddess of divine vengeance who turned Niobe to stone.[61]

In the *Illiad*[62], Homer wrote that Niobe "*stands among the crags in the untrodden hills of Sipylos, where people say the Nymphs, when they have been dancing on the banks of Achelous, lay themselves down to sleep. There Niobe, in marble, broods on the desolation that the gods dealt out to her.*"

On Mount Sipylos there is a limestone rock which is said to be Queen Niobe. When it rains, the rock appears to weep as the water seeps through the porous rock.

The Slaying of Orion

There are conflicting stories about the relationship between the giant Orion and Artemis. In some of the stories Orion is a hunting companion of Artemis, who gets killed by Gaia's scorpion for boasting that he could kill anything upon the earth, in others Artemis and Orion seems to have a friendlier relationship.

---

[60] *Pausanias 9.5.9.*
[61] *Dionysiaca 48.395.*
[62] *Illiad 24:612ff.*

According to Ovid the scorpion first tried to kill Leto, but Orion stepped in its way to save Leto and was killed in the process. Leto then placed him amongst the stars as a reward for saving her life.[63]

Apollodorus tells the story of how Artemis killed Orion on Delos, where he was taken by Aphrodite. Apollodorus gave two possible reasons for this killing, saying that it was either because Orion challenged Artemis to a discus match (presumably claiming to be better than the goddess), or alternatively because he forced himself on Opis, one of Artemis' virgin attendants.[64]

A Roman version of the story, which centres around the creation of the constellation of Scorpio, substitutes Diana for Artemis and introduces a romantic element. This story, which was recounted by Hyginus in his *Astronomica*, tells the story of how Tellus (Gaia) sent the Scorpio to kill Orion for boasting to Diana (Artemis) and Latona (Leto) that he could kill anything that the Earth produced.

Following the death of Orion, Jove (Zeus) placed the Scorpion amongst the stars in remembrance of the courage of both parties, as a lesson to mankind to not be too full of self confidence. Diana (Artemis), mourning the loss of Orion, asked Jove (Zeus) to grant her the same favour as he had given to Tellus (Gaia). For this reason Jove (Zeus) created the Orion constellation in such a way that it sets in the night sky whenever Scorpio rises.[65]

In yet a different version of this story, the writer Hyginus tells us that Istrus said that Diana loved Orion and that the two considered getting married. Apollo, brother to Diana did not take this lightly and tried to persuade her, but to no avail. Apollo then tricked her into shooting Orion by daring her that she could not hit a black object in the sea with her arrows, the object being Orion who was swimming in the distance. She was proud of her shooting skills and upon this dare, shot an arrow, piercing Orion's head. His body later washed up upon the shore and Diana grieving his loss placed him amongst the stars, as the constellation of Orion.[66]

---

[63] *Ovid, Fasti 5.493.*
[64] *Apollodorus 1.25.*
[65] *Hyginus, Astronomica 2.26.*
[66] *Hyginus, Astronomica 2.34.*

6. Titles of Artemis

Artemis had a large number of cult titles and epithets by which she was known. By considering these we can gain more insight into the goddess, as they give us a clearer perception of which of her qualities were focused on the most and emphasised by her worshippers.

Additional titles were given to Artemis in relation to her temples and sanctuaries, and in some instances the founders of temples. These are all included in the list below.

Apankhomení (Απανκομενη)
One of the strangest forms of Artemis is undoubtedly that of *Apankhomení*, meaning *the strangled lady*. Pausanias[67] recounts the tale of some children putting a noose around the neck of an Artemis statue and saying they were hanging her. In fear the men of the village stoned the children to death, but Artemis was furious with the adults for killing the children (of whom certainly the girls would have been under her protection). Artemis made the women suffer with disease, and in atonement the cult of the *Hanging Artemis* of Kaphya was instituted to appease her.

It is interesting to note that the maiden Aspalis committed suicide by hanging herself to preserve her virginity, which may have been a symbolic choice of death to associate herself with Artemis in this guise. Another instance of suicide by hanging was described by Lactantius in his commentary on the *Thebaid of Statius*, where he describes the dancing maidens at Karyai fearing they would be molested, taking shelter in a tree and hanging themselves from the branches.[68]

Artemis Adrasteia (Αδραστεια)
Suidas referenced Demestrios of Skepsis saying that a man called Adrastos established the cult of *Artemis Adrasteia*, meaning *of Adrastos*.[69]

---

[67] *Pausanias 8.23.6.*
[68] *Lactantius, ad Statius Thebaid, 4.225.*
[69] *Suidas, Adrasteia.*

Artemis Agoraia (Αγοραια)

Pausanias refers to an altar of *Artemis Agoraia*, meaning *of the market*, at the village of Olympia.[70]

Artemis Agrotera (Αγροτερα)

This title, meaning *the Huntress* or *of the wilds*, was one of the most commonly used for Artemis in the *Illiad*, and is also found in Pausanias.[71] It emphasizes her preference for being out in the wilds, hunting on mountains and in forests. The temple of *Artemis Agrotera* in Athens had a statue of Artemis with her bow, as it was said to be the first place where she hunted when she arrived from Delos.[72] A temple in Hyllos in Megara was dedicated to *Artemis Agrotera* and *Apollo Agraios* (*the hunter*) by Alkathoos after killing the Kithaironian lion.[73]

Artemis Aiginaií (Αιγιναιη)

There was a sanctuary at Sparta of *Artemis Aiginaií*, meaning *of Aiginia* (the island).[74]

Artemis Aithopia (ΑιΘοπια)

This title, meaning *burning faced one*, was found on a statue of Artemis at her temple on the Island of Lesbos.

Artemis Aitolí (Αιτωλη)

At Naupaktos in Ozolian Lokris there was a sanctuary of *Artemis Aitolí*, meaning *of Aitolia*. The white marble statue there was of Artemis hurling a javelin.[75] Strabo also refers to a precinct sacred to *Artemis Aitolí* amongst the Henetoi of Northern Italy, where wild animals were said to become tame and deer herded with wolves.[76]

Artemis Alpheiaia (Αλφειαια)

There was a sacred precinct to *Artemis Alpheiaia*, meaning *of the river Alpheios*, at the village of Letrinoi near the outlet of the river in Elis in

---

[70] *Pausanias 5.15.4.*
[71] *Pausanias 1.19.6, see also 2.3.5, & 5.15.8, & 7.26.3, & 7.26.11, & 8.32.4.*
[72] *Pausanias 1.19.6.*
[73] *Pausanias 1.41.3.*
[74] *Pausanias 3.14.2.*
[75] *Pausanias 10.38.12.*
[76] *Strabo 5.1.9.*

southern Greece. Strabo describes there being two very famous paintings there, *Artemis borne aloft on a griffin* by Aregon, and *Capture of Troy* by Kleanthes.[77]

Artemis Amarysií (Αμαρυσιη)
At the town of Amarynthos in Euboia there was a temple to *Artemis Amarysií,* meaning *of Amarynthos*, where a major festival was celebrated in her honour.[78] Strabo describes carvings on the pillar of the temple showing the festival procession containing three thousand soldiers, six hundred horsemen and sixty chariots.[79]

Artemis Anaeitis (Αναιιτις)
Pausanias mentions the Lydians having a shrine of *Artemis Anaeitis* but says nothing that helps explain this.[80]

Artemis Ariste (Αριστε)
Pausanias refers to a wooden image of Artemis surnamed Ariste, meaning *best*, in the precinct of Artemis in Athens.[81]

Artemis Aristiboule (Αριστηβουλε)
Plutarch records that the Athenian leader Themistokles built a temple to *Artemis Aristiboule*, meaning *the best counseller*.[82] Sacrifices of criminals were also made to *Artemis Aristiboule*. Initially this custom was performed to Kronos on the sixth of Metageitnion, but it was changed to a sacrifice to Artemis (the sixth of each month being her sacred day). The condemned man was given wine to drink and then slain.[83]

Artemis Astrateia (Αστρατεια)
Pausanias[84] describes this title, meaning *stayed their advance*, referring to the shrine of Artemis at Pyrrhikhos, where the Amazons stayed their advance (i.e. stopped).

---

[77] *Strabo 8.3.12.*
[78] *Pausanias 1.31.5.*
[79] *Strabo 10.1.10.*
[80] *Pausanias 3.16.7.*
[81] *Pausanias 1.29.2.*
[82] *Plutarch, Themistocles 22.1.*
[83] *Porphyry, De abstinentia.*
[84] *Pausanias 3.25.3.*

Artemis Astyríní (Αστυρηνη)
This title, meaning *of Astyra*, refers to the worship of Artemis at the small town of Astyra in Troia, in Anatolia.[85]

Artemis Basileis (Βασιλεις)
Herodotus[86] refers to Thracian and Paionian women sacrificing to *Artemis Basileis*, meaning *the royal Artemis*.

Artemis Brauronia (Βραυρωνια)
One of the main titles of Artemis, meaning *of Brauron*. More information on this title and the associated rites and temple can be found in the section *Artemis of Brauron* in chapter 3 *Temples & Sanctuaries of Artemis*.

Artemis Colaenis (Χολαενισ)
In Aristophanes' play *The Birds*, Artemis is referred to as *Artemis Colaenis*, meaning *of Colaenis*, an Athenian king said to be a descendant of Hermes who erected a temple to Artemis in this name.

Artemis Daphnaií (Δαφναιη)
A sanctuary to Artemis Daphnaií, meaning *of the laurel*, was situated in Hypsous in Lacedaimonia.[87] Strabo also mentions an annual festival to Artemis as Daphnaií and Elaphiaia at Olympia.[88]

Artemis Dereatis (Δερεατις)
An image of *Artemis Dereatis*, meaning *of Dereion*, was set up in the open at Dereion in Lacedaimonia, next to a spring called Anonos.[89]

Artemis Eileithyia (Ειλειθυια)
This title of Eileithyia, used in *Orphic Hymn 2*, meaning *helping goddess*, was one given to a group of unnamed divine attendants who assisted in childbirth, and which was also given to Artemis in her role of divine midwife assisting in the easing of births.

---

[85] *Strabo 13.1.51 & 13.1.65.*
[86] *Herodotus 4.33.*
[87] *Pausanias 3.24.9.*
[88] *Strabo 8.3.12.*
[89] *Pausanias 3.20.7.*

This title is also used for Hera, and Homer refers to the Eileithyiai as daughters of Hera[90] and it is also shared with a number of other goddesses. In *Orphic Hymn 2*, which is to Prothyraia, we see that this obscure name is equated to Artemis Eileithyia.

Artemis Elaphiaia (Ελαφιαια)
Pausanias[91] mentions this title of Artemis, meaning *of the deer*, in reference to her hunting of them. Strabo also mentions an annual festival to Artemis Elaphiaia at Olympia.[92]

Artemis Enodia (Ενοδια)
A temple to Artemis Enodia, meaning *of the road*, was established at Pherai around 700 BCE. This title is more commonly associated with the goddess Hekate.

Artemis Ephesia (Εφεσια)
A major title of Artemis, meaning *of Ephesus*. More information on this title and the associated rites and temple can be found in the section *Artemis of Ephesus* in chapter 3 *Temples & Sanctuaries of Artemis*.

Artemis Eukleia (Ευκλεια)
Pausanias told of the temple in Thebes to Artemis Eukleia, meaning *of fair fame* or *of good repute*, which had a stone lion statue in front of it, said to have been dedicated by Herakles after his victory over the Orkhomenians.[93]

Plutarch wrote some years before this, saying that though Eukleia was regarded as Artemis, that some said she was the daughter of Herakles and Myrto, who died a virgin and was immortalised. She received divine honors from the Boiotians and Lokrians, with an altar and image in every market place, being given preliminary sacrifices by would-be brides and bridegrooms as the goddess of good repute.[94]

[90] *Illiad 11.270.*
[91] *Pausanias 6.22.8.*
[92] *Strabo 8.3.12.*
[93] *Pausanias 9.17.1.*
[94] *Plutarch, Aristides 20.5.*

Xenophon wrote of how a mixed band of Athenians, Argives and Boeotians attacked Thebes on the last day of the festival to Artemis Eukleia in 392 BCE to ensure they killed more people. They were driven away by the young Theban men.[95]

Artemis Eurynomi (Ευρυνωμη)

Pausanias[96] refers to Artemis by this title, meaning *of the broad pasture*, in respect of a shrine to her at Phigalia in Arcadia surrounded by cypress trees.

Artemis Eustephanos Keladeine (Ευστεφανος Κελαδεινη)

The *Illiad* describes Artemis as Eustephanos Keladeine, meaning *sweet-garlanded lady of clamours*, when she complains to Zeus of having been hit by Hera.[97]

Artemis Heleia ('Ηελεια)

Strabo gives this title, meaning *of the marsh*, for Artemis at her temple in the village of Helos in Southern Greece.[98]

Artemis Hemere ('Ηεμερε)

In *Hymn 3 to Artemis*, Callimachus refers to Artemis Hemere, meaning *the gentle* or *she who soothes*, as the aspect of a shrine at Lousa dedicated to her by Proitos for returning his daughters safely to him calmed of their wild spirits. Pausanias also refers to this shrine.[99]

Artemis Hiereia ('Ηιερεια)

A sanctuary at Oresthasion in Arcadia was dedicated to Artemis Hiereia, meaning *priestess*.[100]

Artemis Hígemoní ('Ηγεμονη)

A sanctuary to Artemis Hígemoní, meaning *the leader*, was established in Sparta.[101] The hero Khronios set up a sanctuary to Artemis Higemoni at Tegea in Arcadia, after killing Aristomelidas, the

---

[95] *Xenophon, The Hellenica.*
[96] *Pausanias 8.41.4.*
[97] *Illiad 21.470.*
[98] *Strabo 8.3.25.*
[99] *Pausanias 8.18.8.*
[100] *Pausanias 8.44.2.*
[101] *Pausanias 3.14.6, also 8.37.1.*

despotic ruler of Orkhomenos, at the behest of Artemis for causing a maiden to commit suicide.[102]

Artemis Hymnia ('Ψμνια)
Pausanias refers to a sanctuary of Artemis Hymnia, meaning *of hymns*, on the border of Orkhomenos in Arcadia, who he says was worshipped by the Arcadians from the earliest times.[103] He also mentions an annual festival held to her there,[104] and declaresthat it was the custom for the priests of Artemis Hymnia to live their lives in purity, abstaining from sex and washing, and not entering any private homes.[105]

Artemis Iokheaira (Ιοχεαιρα)
Hesiod refers to Artemis with this title, meaning *delighter in arrows*, when describing her and Apollo as children of Zeus, and it is also found in the *Odyssey*[106] and *Homeric Hymn 3 to Apollo*.[107]

Artemis Iphigeneia (Ιφιγενεια)
There was a sanctuary at Hermione in Argolis of Artemis Iphigeneia, referring to the goddess/heroine who was a companion of Artemis, which may have been in honour of both of them.[108]

Artemis Issoria (Ισσωρια)
Pausanias refers to a sanctuary of *Artemis Issoria*, meaning *of Issorion*, at Issorion in Sparta,[109] and also in Teuthrone, both in Lacedaimonia.[110]

Artemis Kalliste (Καλλιστε)
Kalliste meaning *fairest* or *most beautiful*, is used as her surname by Pausanias when he refers to the wooden image of Artemis found with the image of Artemis Ariste, in the precinct of Artemis in Athens.[111]

[102] *Pausanias 8.47.6.*
[103] *Pausanias 8.5.11.*
[104] *Pausanias 8.13.1.*
[105] *Pausanias 8.13.1.*
[106] *Odyssey 6.102.*
[107] *Hesiod, Theogony 918.*
[108] *Pausanias 2.35.1.*
[109] *Pausanias 3.14.2 see also Plutarch's Lives Vol 2.*
[110] *Pausanias 3.25.4.*
[111] *Pausanias 1.29.2, also 8.35.8.*

Artemis Karyatis (Καρυατισ)

At Karyai in Lacedaimonia was an image of Artemis Karyatis, meaning *of the walnut trees*, where an image of Artemis was set out in the open. The area was sacred to Artemis and her Nymphs, and every year the Lacedaimonian maidens would dance and sing chorally there.[112] The term Caryatid, for pillars shaped like female figures, is derived from the Greek *Karyatides*, the dancers of Artemis Karyatis.

Artemis Kedreatis (Κεδρεατις)

This name, meaning *Lady of the Cedar*, refers to an image set in a cedar tree near the old city of Orkhomenos.[113]

Artemis Khryselakatos (Χρυσαλακατος)

This title occurs frequently, in the *Illiad*[114] and *Homeric Hymns* (5 and 27). It means *with shafts of gold*, and refers to her golden arrows, used in the hunt, and also to inflict disease if she was displeased.

Artemis Khrysaoros (Χρυσαορος)

Herodotus mentions this title, meaning *golden-sworded*, referring to the headland of Kynosoura.[115]

Artemis Khrysenios (Χρυσηνιος)

In the *Illiad*[116] Artemis is described by this title, meaning *of the golden reins*, referring to her golden chariot.

Artemis Khrysothronos (Χρυσοθρονος)

The *Odyssey*[117] refers to Artemis by this title, meaning *golden-throned*, which also occurs in the *Illiad*,[118] and hints at solar attributions.

---

[112] *Pausanias 3.10.7.*
[113] *Pausanias 8.13.1.*
[114] *Illiad 16.181.*
[115] *Herodotus 8.77.*
[116] *Illiad 6.205.*
[117] *Odyssey 5.119.*
[118] *Illiad 9.530.*

Artemis Kindyas (Κινδυας)
Strabo mentions a temple of *Artemis Kindyas*, meaning *of Kindye*, near Bargylia in Kos, where Kindye had been, and where the rain was said to fall without ever hitting the temple.[119]

Artemis Knagia (Κναγια)
Knageus was a Spartan hero who was taken prisoner in battle and sold as a slave to the Cretans. He lived in the sanctuary of Artemis there, but ran away with the maiden priestess, who took the image of Artemis with her. They subsequently set up a temple of Artemis Knagia, meaning *of Knageus*, in Sparta.[120] This tale corresponds closely to the theme of the story of Iphigeneia and Orestes.

Artemis Knakalísia (Κνακαλησια)
This title, meaning *of Knakalos,* refers to the worship of Artemis at her sanctuary at Mount Knakalos in Arcadia.[121]

Artemis Knakeatis (Κνακεατις)
Pausanias mentions the ruins of a temple to Artemis Knakeatis near Tegea in Arcadia.[122]

Artemis Kokkoka (Κοκκοκα)
This name has several suggested meanings. It has been suggested as *of the grain*, or *of the pomegranate seed.*[123] Pausanias said he does not know why Artemis is given this surname.[124]

Artemis Kolainis (Κολαινις)
Callimachus records that Artemis had this name, meaning *hornless*, because Agamemnon sacrificed a hornless ram made of wax to her. This resulted in her worship at Amarynthos in Euboia under this title.[125] In the same fragment Callimachus also wrote that the one-eyed and tailless were sacrificed to her.

---

[119] *Strabo 14.2.20.*
[120] *Pausanias 3.18.4, 4.31.7.*
[121] *Pausanias 8.23.3*
[122] *Pausanias 8.53.11.*
[123] *Sexual Culture in Ancient Greece* – Garrison, 2000, p86.
[124] *Pausanias 5.15.7.*
[125] *Callimachus Iambi Frag 6 (from Scholiast on Aristophanes The Birds 873).*

Artemis Koloínís (Κολοηνης)

This title, meaning *of Koloe*, refers to Lake Koloe, formerly known as Lake Gygaia, near Sardis in Lydia. Strabo mentions that the baskets danced at the festivals held here, declaiming this as talking of marvels rather than the truth.[126]

Artemis Kondyleatis (Κονδψλεατισ)

Artemis was known by this title, meaning *of Kondylea*, a place near Kaphya, until the incident of the children putting a noose around the statue's neck and being stoned by the adults. After making reparation the goddess was then worshipped as Apankhomení (*the strangled lady*).[127]

Artemis Kordax (Κορδαξ)

Artemis was well known for her connection with dancing, and this name associates her with the Cordax (or Kordax), a dance from Lydia that was sacred to her.[128]

Artemis Kore (Κορε)

Callimachus refers to Artemis as Kore, or *maiden*, in *Hymn 3 to Artemis*, referring to the shrine set up by Proitos in her honour as Artemis Kore when she returned his maiden daughters who had been wandering the Azanian Hills back to him.

Artemis Koryphaia (Χορψπηαια)

A sanctuary was built on the top of Mount Koryphon in Argolis as Koryphaia, meaning *of the peak*.[129]

Artemis Korythalia (Κορψτηαλια)

This name means, *of the flowering of young branches*, and may refer either to the growth of vegetation, or metaphorically to the growth of children, as the *korythale* was a laurel branch carried ritually before marriage by young women and men.[130] Plutarch also states that one

---

[126] *Strabo 13.4.5.*
[127] *Pausanias 8.23.6.*
[128] *Pausanias 6.22.1.*
[129] *Pausanias 2.28.2.*
[130] See *Choruses of Young Women in Ancient Greece* – Calame, 1997, p170-71.

of Apollo's nurses was called Korythaleia, hinting at Artemis in her role as kourotrophos.[131]

Artemis Laphria (Λαφρια)
Pausanias recounts this title, meaning *of Laphros*, being used after a Phocian hero called Laphros, who set up the image of Artemis at Calydon. After Emperor Augustus had laid waste to Calydon and the whole area of Aitolia around it, the statue of Artemis Laphria was given to the people of Patrai.[132] The festival of Laphria was celebrated annually in honour of Artemis at Patrai.

Artemis Leukophruíní (Λευκοφρυηνη)
Pausanias tells how the Magnesians honoured Artemis as Leukophruíní, meaning *of the white bird*, dedicating a statue to her in this name in her temple in Magnesia,[133] and erecting a bronze statue of her in this name in Athens.[134] Strabo wrote that although the Magnesian temple was inferior in size and quantity of votive offerings to Ephesus, the harmony and skill shown in its building were superior; he also notes it as the third largest temple in Asia after those of Artemis at Ephesus and Apollo at Didymoi.[135]

Artemis Limnaií (Λιμναιη)
This title meaning *Lady of the lake* was used by Pausanias[136] to describe Artemis, but he states it was really a title of Britomartis, another goddess whose worship became subsumed into that of Artemis. However the number of references in his writings to other temples of Artemis Limnaií suggest that this was a common title.[137]

Artemis Lokhia (Λοκηια)
There was a sanctuary of Artemis Lokhia, meaning *helper in childbirth*, at her temple in Delos. Euripides refers to Artemis Lokhia in two of his plays. In *Iphigeneia in Tauris*, Artemis Lokhia is described in a landscape of laurels, olive shoots and palm trees,[138]

---

[131] *Plutarch, Moralia 657.*
[132] *Pausanias 7.18.8.*
[133] *Pausanias 3.18.7.*
[134] *Pausanias 1.26.4, & 3.18.7.*
[135] *Strabo 14.1.40.*
[136] *Pausanias 3.14.2.*
[137] See *Pausanias 2.7.6, 3.23.10, 7.20.7, & 8.53.11.*
[138] *Euripides, Iphigeneia in Tauris, 1097.*

and in *The Suppliants* the mothers of children killed beneath the walls of Thebes weep because their children are no longer under the protection of Artemis Lokhia.[139]

Artemis Lykeií (Λυκειη)
According to Pausanias this name of Lykeií, meaning *of the wolves*, was a surname of Artemis among the Amazons.[140]

Artemis Lykoí (Λυκοη)
A bronze image of the goddess as *Artemis Lykoí*, meaning *of Lykoa*, was set in her temple at Lykoa in Arcadia, under Mount Mainalos.[141]

Artemis Mounykhia (Μουνυχια)
Pausanias refers to a temple of *Artemis Mounykhia*, meaning *of Mounykhia* in the harbour of the port of the same name in Attica.[142] Strabo refers to a temple of *Artemis Mounykhia* founded by Agamemnon at the town of Pygela near Ephesus.[143] Suidas also mentions sacrifice to *Artemis Mounykhia* in Athens during the month of *Mounykhion*.[144]

Artemis Mysia (Μυσια)
Pausanias records that on the road from Sparta to Arcadia was a sanctuary of *Artemis Mysia*, meaning *of Mysia*.[145]

Artemis Nemydia (Νεμυδια)
Strabo mentions a temple of Artemis Nemydia at the village of Teuthia in Elis.[146] It is not known what this name means.

Artemis Orthia (Ορθια)
Pausanias refers to a sanctuary of Artemis on Mount Lykone, as Artemis Orthia, meaning *of the steep*, where marble images of her with her mother Leto and brother Apollo were to be found.[147]

---

[139] *Euripides, Suppliants, 955.*
[140] *Pausanias 2.31.4.*
[141] *Pausanias 8.36.7.*
[142] *Pausanias 1.1.4.*
[143] *Strabo 14.1.20.*
[144] *Suidas, Mounykhion.*
[145] *Pausanias 3.20.9.*
[146] *Strabo 8.3.11.*
[147] *Pausanias 2.24.5*, see also *3.16.7.*

Artemis Orthosia (Ορθοσια)
Herodotus mentions an altar of *Artemis Orthosia*, meaning *of Orthosia* at the city of Byzantion on the Bosporus Strait.[148] Orthosia was a Karyian city in Anatolia.

Artemis Peitho (Πειθω)
A sanctuary at Argos was dedicated to Artemis Peitho, meaning *the persuasive*.[149]

Artemis Pergaia (Περγαια)
This title, meaning *of Perge*, was used at the temple near Perge in Pamphylia. A festival was celebrated there every year[150], and it is mentioned by Callimachus[151], and also with reference to hymns composed by the poetess Damophyle in honour of *Artemis Pergaia*.[152]

Artemis Persia (Περσια)
Artemis Persia, meaning *of Persia* was celebrated at a sanctuary in Lydia.[153]

Artemis Pheraia (Φεραια)
Although this title means *of the beasts*, Pausanias asserts that it originated from an image brought from Pherai in Thessalia.[154]

Artemis Propylaií (Προπυλαιη)
According to Pausanias the Eleusinians had a temple of Artemis Propylaií, meaning *of the gate*.[155] This title was frequently used for the goddess Hekate.

Artemis Proseoia (Προσεοια)
A small temple to Artemis Proseoia was located near the village of Hestiaia in Euboia. It has been suggested that this name means *facing the East*, as this was an eastward facing port.[156]

---

[148] *Herodotus 4.87.*
[149] *Pausanias 2.21.1.*
[150] *Strabo 14.4.2.*
[151] *Callimachus, Hymn 3 to Artemis.*
[152] *Life of Apollonius of Tyana 1.30.*
[153] *Pausanias 7.6.6.*
[154] *Pausanias 2.23.5*, see also *2.10.7.*
[155] *Pausanias 1.38.6.*

Artemis Protothronií (Πρωτοθρονιη)

Pausanias tells of an altar to Artemis Protothronií, meaning *of the first throne*, within a temple of Artemis Ephesia at Amphissa in Phocis.[157]

Artemis Pyronia (Πυρωνια)

Pausanias describes a sanctuary to Artemis Pyronia, meaning *of the fire*, at Mount Krathis in Arcadia, where the people had used fire from the sanctuary in their ceremonies.[158]

Artemis Rhokkaia (Ροκκαια)

This title, meaning *of Rhokkha*, refers to the worship of Artemis at the village of Rhokkha in Crete. Aelian described dogs in Rhokkha going mad and hurling themselves into the sea.[159] Aelian went on to say that boys bitten by these dogs were taken to the temple of Artemis for healing.[160]

Artemis Saronis (Σαρωνις)

This title, meaning *of Saron*, refers to an Argosian hero, who established a sanctuary of Artemis near Troizenos in Argolis, where an annual festival called the Saronia was held.[161] He eventually died chasing a doe which swam into the sea. He followed the doe and drowned, and his body came ashore at the grove of Artemis by the Phoibaian lagoon, where it was buried within the sacred enclosure.[162]

Artemis Sarpedonia (Σαρπεδωνια)

At Pylai in Kilikia (Anatolia) was the temple and oracle of Artemis Sarpedonia, meaning *of Sarpedon*,[163] a Lycian hero, who may have established the temple.

Artemis Selasphoros (Σελασφορος)

Pausanias refers to altars to Artemis Selasphoros, meaning *the light bearer*, in the Attic towns of Phyla and Myrrhinos.[164]

---

[156] *Plutarch, Themistocles 8.1.*
[157] *Pausanias 10.38.6.*
[158] *Pausanias 8.15.8.*
[159] *Aelian, On Animals 12.22.*
[160] *Aelian, on Animals 14.20.*
[161] *Pausanias 2.32.10.*
[162] *Pausanias 2.30.7.*
[163] *Strabo 14.5.19.*
[164] *Pausanias 1.31.4.*

Artemis Skiatis (Σκιατις)

Pausanias refers to a sanctuary of Artemis Skiatis, meaning of Skias, which was said to have been built by the tyrant Aristodemos at Skias near Megalopolis in Arcadia.[165]

Artemis Skythia (Σκυθια)

This title, meaning of Scythia, is referred to in the Life of Apollonius of Tyana. In response to questions from the Egyptian sage Thespesion, Apollonius describes the ritual scourging that was done in honour of Artemis Skythia. The scourging would continue until blood was flowing freely and the blood from the wounds would be smeared on the altar, as prescribed by the oracle.

When asked why the Greeks did not sacrifice people as the Skythoi previously did, Apollonius replied that the Greeks should not adopt in full the manners and customs of barbarians.[166]

Artemis Soteira (Σωτειρα)

This title is often used for Artemis for her aid. Pausanias recounts how the Megarans (people of Megara) named Artemis as Soteira, meaning saviour, after she helped them against the army of General Mardonios, making a bronze image in her honour.[167] Another identical bronze image was set in a temple at Pagai, in Megara.[168] Pausanias also mentions Theseus founding a temple to Artemis Soteira when he returned to Troizenos in Argolis after defeating the Minotaur.[169]

The city of Boiai in Lacedaimonia had a shrine to Artemis Soteira after her help in revealing the site for the city to be built on.[170] Processions for Artemis were begun from the sanctuary of Artemis Soteira by the people of Phigalia in Arcadia.[171] Soteira is another title that was frequently used for the goddess Hekate.

---

[165] Pausanias 8.35.5.
[166] Life of Apollonius of Tyana 6.20.
[167] Pausanias 1.40.2.
[168] Pausanias 1.44.4.
[169] Pausanias 2.31.4.
[170] Pausanias 3.22.12. Other references include 7.27.4, & 8.30.10.
[171] Pausanias 8.39.5.

Artemis Stymphalia (Στυμφαλια)

This title, meaning *of Stymphalos*, refers to Stymphalos, in Arcadia, famed for the Stymphalian birds. Pausanias went into some detail about the sanctuary at Stymphalos, mentioning carvings of the Stymphalian birds near the roof of the temple. He also describes white marble statues of maidens with bird legs standing behind the temple who were known as Stymphalian Nymphs.

Pausanias thought that the celebrations and rites of the festival of *Artemis Stymphalia* were celebrated in a careless manner. This, he tells us, resulted in a log falling into the mouth of the chasm through which the river descended, preventing drainage, flooding the plain and creating the marshes.

Later when a hunter was chasing a deer into the marsh, both the hunter and the hunted were swallowed up by the chasm. The river followed them, drying out the entire plain. Worshippers at Stymphalos subsequently paid far more respect and made more of an effort to honour Artemis properly.[172]

Artemis Tauria (Ταυρια)

Pausanias refers to the old wooden image of Artemis in Brauron as *Artemis Tauria*, meaning *of Tauros*.[173]

Artemis Tauropolos (Ταυροπολος)

Strabo refers to *Artemis Tauropolos*, meaning *of Tauros*, in Skythia, saying that Orestes and Iphigeneia took the rites from there to Komana in Kappadokia (Asia Minor), where she was identified with a Kappadokian goddess.[174] Cassius Dio refers to the statue of Tauric Artemis at Kappadokia and her worship there, giving a date of 68 BCE for his comments.[175]

---

[172] *Pausanias 8.22.7.*
[173] *Pausanias 1.23.7.*
[174] *Strabo 12.2.3.*
[175] *Dio's Rome, 11.*

Artemis Triklaria (Τρικλαρια)
This title of Triklaria, meaning *of the three settlements*, refers to the communal worship of Artemis by the people of three settlements.[176] The temple of Artemis Triklaria at Patrai was defiled by the lovemaking of Lomaitho and Melanippos in the inner sanctuary of the temple (see the section on *Lomaitho and Melanippos*).

Bromia (Βρομια)
This title, meaning *noisy one* or *thunderer*, is found in *Orphic Hymn 36*. It is the female equivalent of Bromios, a title of Dionysus, and emphasises the link between the two of them.

Cynthia (Χψντηια)
Ovid refers to Artemis by this name of Cynthia in his *Fasti*.[177] It is derived from Mount Cynthus on Delos, where Artemis was said to have been born. Athena was also sometimes referred to as Athena Cynthia after her shrine on the same mountain.

Delia (Δελια)
This is another title used by Ovid, meaning *of Delos*, the island of her birth.[178]

Diktynna (Δικτυννα)
Orphic Hymn 36 and Aristophanes both refer to Artemis as Diktynna[179], meaning *of the hunting nets*, which is also the name of the Cretan goddess who was subsumed into the worship of Artemis and subsequently portrayed as one of her hunting companions. This is described by Callimachus in his *Hymn 3 to Artemis*, referring to her as named Diktynna after the "Cretan nymph". Pausanias refers to an annual festival of *Artemis Diktynna* at her temple in Hypsous in Lacedaimonia.[180]

Elaphabolos (Ελαφηβολος)
From *Homeric Hymn 27*, this title means *deer-shooting*, and refers to her role as supreme huntress, and deer, her favourite prey.

---

[176] *Pausanias 7.19.1 and 7.22.11.*
[177] *Ovid, Fasti 2.155, and Metamorphoses 2.414, 7.732.*
[178] *Ovid Fasti 5.493.*
[179] *Aristophanes, Frogs 1358.*
[180] *Pausanias 3.24.9, see also 10.36.5.*

Hekaerge ('Εκαεργε)

This title of Artemis, meaning *far-working*, is also the name of one of her attendants. Callimachus refers to Hekaerge in one place as Artemis,[181] and in another as one of the daughters of Boreas (the North Wind).[182]

Hekatebolon Iokheaira ('Εκατηβολον Ιοχεαιρα)

From *Homeric Hymn 9*, this title means *far-shooting delighter in arrows*. Arrows are frequently mentioned in Artemis' titles, showing how strongly they were associated with her.

Heurippa ('Ευριππα)

This name, meaning *horse-finder*, was said to come from Odysseus, who set up a sanctuary to Artemis at Pheneos in Arcadia after finding his lost mares there.[183]

Iokheaira (Ιοχεαιρα)

From *Homeric Hymn 27*, and meaning *delighter in arrows*, this title refers to her archery, and was sometimes used in conjunction with other titles, such as Hekatebolon Iokheaira and Theroskopos Iokheaira.

Keladeine (Κελαδεινη)

In the *Illiad*[184] and *Homeric Hymn 27*, Artemis was given this title meaning *strong voiced*, and referring to Artemis as a singer, emphasizing her musical ability.

Khitone (Χιτοηε)

Found in Callimachus *Hymn 3 to Artemis*, this title means *goddess of the tunic*, and refers to the short hunting tunic worn by Artemis, known as a khitone.

Kourotrophos (Κουροτροφος)

This title, meaning *child's nurse*, was sometimes used for Artemis, but was also used for the goddesses Hekate and Gaia.

---

[181] *Callimachus, Hymn 4 to Delos.*
[182] *Callimachus, Hymn 4 to Delos.*
[183] *Pausanias 8.14.5.*
[184] *Illiad 16.181.*

Limenoskope (Λιμενοσκοπε)

Callimachus *Hymn 3 to Artemis* describes her as Limenoskope, meaning *watcher of harbours*, referring to her role as guardian of harbours previously mentioned in the same hymn.

Lítois (Λητωις)

This name, meaning *daughter of Leto*, is found in Ovid.[185]

Lygodesmí (Λυγοδεσμη)

This title was given to the statue found by Astrabakos and Alopekos, and established in the shrine at Ortygia, and means *willow-bound*, due to the image being found in a thicket of willow.[186]

Orsilokhia (Ορσιλοχια)

Another title referring to her role in aiding childbirth, meaning *helper in childbirth*. Antoninus Liberalis refers to this title as being the name given to Iphigeneia when she became the immortal companion of Akhilleus.[187]

Paidotrophos (Παιδοτροφος)

There was a temple to Artemis as Paidotrophos, meaning *child nurse*, at Korone in Messenia.[188]

Parthenon Aidoine (παρθενονΑιδοιον)

From *Homeric Hymn 27*, this title meaning *revered virgin* emphasises the virginal nature of Artemis.

Parthenos (Παρθενος)

Artemis was referred to by Callimachus as Parthenos, meaning *virgin*.[189] There was a temple of Artemis Parthenos on the island of Leros.

---

[185] *Ovid, Metamorphoses 7.384.*
[186] *Pausanias 3.16.7.*
[187] *Antoninus Liberalis, Metamorphoses, 27.*
[188] *Pausanias 4.34.6.*
[189] *Callimachus, Hymn 3 to Artemis.*

Parthenos Iokheaira (παρθενος Ιοχεαιρα)

This title is found in *Homeric Hymn 9*, meaning *the virgin who delights in arrows*, emphasizing both her virginal nature and her favourite hunting tools, the bow and arrow.

Phoebe (Φωεβε)

This title, meaning *light*, was used by Ovid[190] and Aristophanes,[191] and also emphasised the link with her twin brother Apollo, who was known as Phoebus, the male form of *light*. There was also a Titan goddess called Phoebe, who was the mother of Asteria and Leto, and hence the grandmother of Artemis and Apollo. The Titan Phoebe was originally the goddess of the Delphic Oracle, which Apollo subsequently took over after the killing of the Python.

Phosphorus (Φωσφορος)

The title, meaning *light-bringer* is found in Callimachus *Hymn 3 to Artemis*, where she demands the title from Zeus. It is a title she shared with Hekate. Pausanias also refers to a statue of Artemis Phosphorus in the sanctuary of Asclepius in Messene.[192]

Potna Thea (Ποτνα Θεα)

Artemis is mentioned in the *Odyssey* as Potna Thea, meaning *goddess queen*.[193]

Potnia Theron (Πωτνια Θερων)

Artemis is described in the *Illiad* as Potnia Theron, meaning *Queen of wild beasts*. This title suggests both her role as Lady of the Animals and also her favoured activity of hunting. It is an ancient title of the nameless *Minoan Lady of the Beasts* which was later assumed by Artemis.

Potnia is a Mycenaean word which was adopted for use by the ancient Greeks and can be translated as *Lady, Mistress* or *Queen*. Regardless of what the Minoans may have called her it is interesting to note that a similar goddess was worshipped throughout the Aegean

---

[190] *Ovid, Metamorphoses 2.414, and Fasti 2.155.*
[191] *Aristophanes, Lysistrata.*
[192] *Pausanias 4.31.10.*
[193] *Odyssey 20.60.*

basin and the ancient near East, which may provide further clues to her origins.

Potnia Theron
This image is based on a depiction of the Lady of the Beast on a Boeotian Amphora from around 680 BCE. It is not unlike that depicted on a Minoan seal which was discovered by Sir Arthur Evans in 1903 on Crete.

Theroskopos Iokheaira (Θηροσκοπος Ιοχεαιρα)
The meaning of this title from *Homeric Hymn 27, the huntress who delights in arrows*, is self-explanatory.

Tityoktone (Τιτψοκτονε)
This title, meaning *slayer of Tityos*, refers to Artemis killing the giant of this name when he tried to molest her mother Leto.[194]

---

[194] *Callimachus, Hymn 3 to Artemis.*

7. Virgin Goddess

Wonder what young intruder dares to sing
In these still haunts, where never foot of man
Should tread at evening, lest he chance to spy
The marble limbs of Artemis and all her company

Oscar Wilde, The Garden of Eros, 1881

Artemis declared as a child that she would remain forever virgin. This is reflected in descriptions of her and several of her titles. She is Hagní Parthenos, *the pure virgin*; Aidoios parthenos, *the revered virgin*; and Parthenos Iokheaira, *the virgin who delights in arrows*.

Artemis' virginity is a major part of her character and she prized the virginity of her attendants, which was illustrated by the severe punishments she effected on those who lost their virginity, regardless of the cause, usually rape by a god. This clearly demonstrates that virginity referred to a complete absence of sexual activity, and of never having experienced sex, not being unmarried, as some people have suggested.

Artemis, together with the virgin goddess of wisdom, Athena and the virgin goddess of the hearth, Hestia, had immunity from the powers of the goddess of love, Aphrodite. Homer wrote that laughter-loving Aphrodite could never tame Artemis in love, saying that the huntress loved archery and slaying of wild beasts in the mountains. [195]

Eros, the god of love was also unable to affect Artemis with his arrows of love, Sappho went as far as to say that Eros never approached her. [196]

Artemis was the unattainable and ultimate trophy, as both a sworn virgin and effective warrior it was dangerous for both gods and mortals to attempt forcing their adorations onto her. Yet, many mortals and gods did fall in love or lust with her.

---

[195] *Homeric Hymn 5 to Aphrodite, 6.*
[196] *Greek Lyric I Sappho Frag 34.*

One of these, Alpheios, a river god, fell in love with Artemis and decided to try and molest her at an all-night gathering she was holding with her nymphs. Artemis suspected that Alpheios would try this, so she smeared her face with mud and made all the other nymphs do likewise. Frustrated at not being able to recognize Artemis, Alpheios gave up and left.[197]

Aristophanes also stressed the chastity of Artemis, with the chorus of women singing of it in his play *Thesmophoriazusae*. Euripides likewise emphasised this point, calling her *"most virginal"*.[198]

As well as punishing those of her companions who lost their virginity, Artemis also did her best to protect those who were threatened. Hence she turned the Arcadian nymphs Arethousa and Syrinx into a spring and reeds respectively to save them, and the nymph Amethyst into a rock to save her.

In the case of the young prince Hippolytus who had devoted his chaste life to her, and was killed through the machinations of Aphrodite, Artemis persuaded the god of healing Asclepius to bring him back to life, and he became her temple attendant at Aricia in Italy.

Some modern writers have suggested that sacred prostitution occurred at the temple of Artemis at Ephesus. However none of the classical writers even hint at this, nor is there any evidence amongst the thousands of Greek and Latin inscriptions found at Ephesus.

If we consider the development of the worship at Ephesus, when Artemis became the dominant goddess, even considering any other goddesses she may have subsumed into her worship, the sacred virgin became pre-eminent, not the sacred prostitute. Looking at inscriptions from Ephesus, the references to priestesses list them as "daughter of" rather than "wife of". This indicates an unmarried and therefore virginal status in those who served Artemis at this temple.

---

[197] *Pausanias 6.22.8.*
[198] *Euripides, Hippolytus.*

8. Goddess of Women

Although most Greek goddesses had some link with childbirth, Artemis was particularly associated with the role of divine midwife. Within moments of her birth she assisted her mother Leto with the birth of her twin brother Apollo, though she was a baby herself.[199]

Artemis was particularly associated with birth itself as the protectress of newborn children, as Orsilokhia which means *helper of childbirth*. She was invoked as *Artemis Orsilokhia* during labour to protect the newborn child.

Callimachus, in his *Hymn 3 to Artemis*[200] suggests that Leto had a trouble and pain free time when she gave birth to Artemis, this points to yet another reason why Artemis should be favoured by women making petitions for a trouble free birth.

Artemis shared the title of Eileithyia, or *helping goddess*, with a number of other goddesses and divine midwives. Although this is a title which was strongly associated with Artemis, the Greek writer Homer named Eileithyia as the goddess of birth-pain, but also wrote about many other Eileithyiai, whom he named as the daughters of Hera. Hesiod also suggested that Eileithyia was the daughter or Zeus and Hera.

It is worth noting that there was a well established cult of the goddess Eileithyia in Crete, centred around the locations of Lato and Eleutherna. Offerings found in caves at Amnisos and at Inatos demonstrate that she was a popular deity there, who flourished throughout the Hellenistic and Roman periods.

Artemis delivered the babies of the Titan Aura, even though she had been angry at her for verbally abusing Artemis and also for becoming pregnant after her rape by Dionysus. And she would perhaps have been more forgiving if Aura had not immediately eaten one of her own babies.[201]

---

[199] *Apollodorus 1.21.*
[200] *Callimachus, Hymn 3 to Artemis.*
[201] *Dionysiaca 48.848.*

Artemis was also said to give particularly easy childbirth at the full moon, a time when animals were thought to have an easier labour.[202]

Artemis and Apollo were both the protectors of children. Hesiod wrote that they were assisted in this role - Artemis by the Sea Nymphs called Oceanides (Clouds) to look after girls and Apollo by the Potamoi (Rivers) to look after boys. However Artemis alone was usually regarded as the protector of the baby from its birth through to weaning, as Kourotrophos or *child's nurse*, and Paidotrophos, *nurse of children*, and likewise was the protector of infant animals.

Votive offerings to Artemis as Kourotrophos have been found at sanctuaries like that at Orthia. These were made of ivory and depicted Artemis, sometimes with attendant birth goddesses (Eileithyiai).

A girl would be under the protection of Artemis until her consecration into womanhood. On reaching maturity a girl would be rededicated to Hera, as goddess of marriage, and Aphrodite, as goddess of love. Offerings would then be made by the young girls to Artemis, honouring her and thanking her for taking care of them.

At some coming of age ceremonies girls would dedicate a lock of their hair to Artemis for the same reason.[203] It has been suggested that the lock of hair symbolised the virginity that the girl would be leaving behind.[204]

The connection of the clothes with Artemis is mentioned with regard to lingerie and also to the clothes of women who died in childbirth.

> *"Virgins about to have sex dedicated their virginal lingerie to Artemis."*[205]

---

[202] *Greek Lyric I Alcaeus Frag 390 (from Scholiast on Illiad).*
[203] See e.g. *Apollodorus 6.276, Pausanias 1.43.4.*
[204] See e.g. *Sacred Marriage in the Rituals of Greek Religion* - Aphrodite Avagianou, 1991, 3 , and *Marriage to Death: The Conflation of Wedding and Funeral Rituals in Greek Tragedy* - Rush Rehm, 1994.
[205] *Suidas, Lysizonos gune.*

Iphigeneia is described as receiving the clothes of women who died in childbirth.[206] At times Iphigeneia is described as an aspect of Artemis and at other times as a companion to Artemis.

By 7th century BCE Iphigeneia had become a companion of Artemis. She was the daughter of Agamemnon, who had angered Artemis by killing a deer and then boasting he was a better hunter than her. Artemis calmed the wind to prevent his fleet leaving for Troy, and to propitiate her Agamemnon was advised to sacrifice his daughter Iphigeneia. He did so, but at the last moment Artemis took pity and substituted a deer in her place, taking Iphigeneia as one of her companions.[207]

---

[206] *Euripides, Iphigeneia in Tauris*, see also *The Temple Legends of Arkteia* – William Sale, in *Rheinisches Museum für Philologie Volume 1:265-84*, 1975.
[207] *Proclus, Chrestomathia.*

9. Lady of the Hunt & Wild Animals

"Praise Artemis also, the maiden huntress, she who wanders on the mountains and through the woods."[208]

Artemis is the goddess of the hunt, whose favourite pursuit is the exercising of her skill as a huntress. She is Theroskopos (*hunter of wild beasts*) and Khitone (*goddess who wears the short hunting tunic*). The Eleans were thought to call her *Artemis Elaphiaia* after her pursuit of hunting deer [*elaphos*].[209] This theme occurs repeatedly, such as in the *Orphic Hymns*, where she was described as the *foe of the stag*.[210]

Artemis was extremely good at getting what she wanted from her father Zeus. As a child she asked him to give her arrows and a bow to slay wild animals, and the mountains to hunt and dwell on.[211]

Many of her titles refer to her skill with her bow, the main instrument of the hunt. She is Artemis Iokheaira [*delighting in arrows*] and Theroskopos Iokheaira [*the huntress who delights in arrows*] ranging the mountains taking her pleasure killing the boars and the running deer.[212]

"Artemis Khryselakatos loves archery and the slaying of wild beasts in the mountains."[213]

Callimachus made frequent reference to Artemis' skill with the bow in his hymns to her: *"whose study is the bow and the shooting of hares and the spacious dance and sport upon the mountains."*, and again when he wrote, *"And how often goddess, did you make trial of thy silver bow?"*[214]

---

[208] *Aristophanes, Thesmophoriazusae 114.*
[209] *Pausanias 6.22.8.*
[210] *Orphic Hymn 36 to Artemis.*
[211] *Callimachus, Hymn 3 to Artemis.*
[212] *Odyssey 6:102.*
[213] *Homeric Hymn 5 to Aphrodite.*
[214] *Callimachus, Hymn 3 to Artemis.*

Many of the depictions of Artemis with animals show her holding one in each hand, either by their necks or hind-paws. This is the sort of position we would associate with carrying game, and may be indicative of her role as goddess of the hunt rather than as goddess of animals.

As a goddess of the hunt Artemis did not always hunt alone. At times she was accompanied by attendants, by her pack of hunting hounds or by the beautiful god of wine and wildness Dionysus, [215] who was one of her closest friends amongst the gods.

> "Stag-hunter Artemis, on the hills thou dost eagerly hunt with fawn-killing Dionysus." [216]

Artemis also hunted fish, as implied by the use of the title Diktynna (*of the nets*), and seen in the Homeric Hymns, where it says: *"[Artemis] draws her golden bow ... The tops of the high mountains tremble ... and the sea also where fishes shoal."* [217]

Artemis was extremely proud of her hunting ability and confident in her supremacy, as would be expected for a goddess who was the patron of hunting. [218] When King Agamemnon boasted he was a better hunter than Artemis, the goddess prevented the Greek fleet from sailing for Troy. Only by offering his daughter as a sacrifice did Agamemnon appease Artemis, who snatched her up and substituted a deer as the killing blow was made (in some versions of the tale Artemis places a bull in her place rather than a deer).

Another hunter, Broteas, son of King Tantalos, (and brother of Niobe) did not honour Artemis, and boasted of his ability, so Artemis made him kill himself by burning himself to death. [219] And as has already been mentioned, in some versions of the tale Artemis killed the giant Orion for claiming to be better at hunting than her.

Artemis was a goddess of the hunt, and also of the wild animals that she hunted. She demonstrated the principles of conservation by

---

[215] *Pindar, Dithyrambs: Heracles the Bold.*
[216] *Dionysiaca 44:198.*
[217] *Homeric Hymn 27 to Artemis.*
[218] *Xenophon, Cynegeticus, 1.*
[219] *Apollodorus E2.2.*

being the protectress of young animals, ensuring the propagation of the species. References were frequently made to Artemis in regard to this role. Hence she is *Artemis sovereign of all creatures,*[220] and *Artemis Agrotera [of the wilderness], Potnia Theron [Lady of wild beasts].*[221]

In his manual for hunters, Xenophon describes the prayer the hunter spoke as he released the hunting hounds, *"To thee thy share of this chase, Lord Apollo; and thine to thee, O Huntress Queen!"*[222]

As well as protecting young animals Artemis also protected their mothers, and hunting female animals could have fatal consequences. On one occasion a hunter called Saron of Troizenos was chasing a doe when it swam into the sea. He drowned and his body washed up at the grove of Artemis at the Phoibaian lagoon.[223] Even Saron's earlier good deeds in setting up a temple to Artemis counted for nothing when he broke this hunting taboo.

It was said that wild animals would behave as if they were tame when they were within the boundaries of a temple of Artemis, recognizing its powers of sanctuary. Strabo records this, describing how deer herded with wolves, and allowed people to stroke them.[224]

Additionally animals would find their way to her sacred places to give birth to their young, recognising this quality of sacred protection from the mistress of the animals.[225]

Those who had killed animals and were uncertain as to the favour of the goddess were wise to propitiate her quickly rather than risk her wrath. Both Hippolytus and Alkathoos are described as building temples to Artemis after slaying wild beasts.[226]

Sometimes choosing one goddess in preference to another had its consequences, as the maiden Polyphonte found out. This princess of

---

[220] *Dionysiaca 11:344.*
[221] *Illiad 21:470.*
[222] *Xenophon, Cynegeticus, 20.*
[223] *Pausanias 2.30.7.*
[224] *Strabo 5.1.9.*
[225] *Strabo 14.1.29.*
[226] *Pausanias 2.31.4.*

the Triballoi tribe of Thrace in Northern Greece was a hunting companion of Artemis, having scorned love and Aphrodite.

In revenge Aphrodite made Polyphonte go mad and make love with a bear. Artemis was disgusted by this and turned the other animals against her, killing her.[227]

A number of animals were considered particularly sacred to Artemis. Chief amongst these were the deer, the dog and the bear, but they also included the boar, the hare and possibly the lion. Several birds were also considered sacred to her, including the partridge, quail and buzzard.

Artemis & Bears

The bear was especially sacred to Artemis, both as the creature and also as the stellar constellation of Ursa Major, the Great Bear. Killing her sacred bears was the most certain way of bringing down Artemis' wrath, as the Athenians found out on two separate occasions.

When the Athenians killed a female bear which appeared in the shrine of Artemis at Mounykhia in Attica the goddess caused a famine to strike them.[228]

On another occasion a tame she-bear that played with the virgins at the sanctuary at Brauron scratched one of the girls after being provoked. The girl's brothers speared the she-bear and killed it, angering Artemis, who sent a pestilential sickness upon the Athenians.

When the Athenians consulted an oracle they were told the girls would hereafter have to play the part of the she-bear in the rites performed at Brauron as the blood-price to atone for killing the bear.[229]

As her cult animal, the bear was especially celebrated in the rites of Artemis. Young girls between the ages of five and fifteen (scholars

---

[227] *Antoninus Liberalis, Metamorphoses, 21.*
[228] *Suidas, Embaros eimi.*
[229] *Suidas, Arktos e Brauroniois.*

seem to disagree on the exact age) had to partake in rites where they dressed up in saffron robes and acted as bears.

> *"The Athenians decreed that no virgin might be given in marriage to a man if she hadn't previously played the bear for the goddess."*[230]

A charm from the Greek Magical Papyri called on Artemis as the Great Bear to assist the magician in achieving their goal, whatever that may be.

> *"Bear, Bear, you who rule the heaven, the stars, and the whole world; you who make the axis turn and control the whole cosmic system by force and compulsion;*
> *I appeal to you, imploring and supplicating that you may do the NN thing, because I call upon you with your holy names at which your deity rejoices, names which you are not able to ignore: Brimō, earth-breaker, chief huntress, Baubo Aumōr Amōr Amōr lēa [shooter] of deer Amam Aphrou Ma, universal queen, queen of wishes, Amama, well-bedded, Dardanian, all-seeing, night-running, man-attacker, man-subduer, man-summoner, man-conqueror, Lichrissa Phaessa, O aerial one, O strong one, O song and dance, guard, spy, delight, delicate, protector, adamant, adamantine, O Damnameneia, Brexerikandara, most high, taurian, unutterable, fire-bodied, light-giving, sharply armed. Do such and such things."*[231]

Artemis & Birds

Unsurprisingly ground birds that could be hunted were particularly popular with Artemis. Hence we find Aelian recording that the partridge (*perdix*) was the darling of Artemis[232] The quail (*ortyx*) was sacred to both Artemis and her mother Leto. The island of Artemis' birth, Delos, was previously named Ortygia after the quail.

---

[230] *Suidas, Arktos e Brauroniois .*
[231] *PGM VII:686-702.*
[232] *Aelian, On Animals 10.35.*

Artemis & The Swan
This image is based on a 5ᵗʰ century BCE vase image, showing artemis feeding a large bird, bow and arrows visible on her back.

Another ground-bird, the guinea-fowl (*meleagris*), featured in one of the stories of Artemis and her wrath. Artemis transformed the Meleagrides, princesses of Aitolia into guinea hens. The princesses were mourning the death of their brother at the hands of Artemis as a result of their father King Oineus' behaviour towards the goddess and she felt sorry for them and so transformed them.[233]

As the goddess of the hunt, it is to be expected that at least one bird of prey should be sacred to her. Aelian describes the buzzard (*triorkhes*), as being sacred to Artemis[234]

Aristophanes associated the goldfinch with Artemis in his play *The Birds*, where the priest said: *"Pray to the swan of Delos [Apollo], to Latona the mother of quails [Leto], and to Artemis, the goldfinch."*

In this context, where Apollo is associated with the swan, it is interesting that a vase image dating to the 5th century BCE shows Artemis feeding a swan, with her bow and quiver visible on her back.[235]

The swan is further associated with Apollo in a legend that tells how Apollo flew on the back of a swan to Hyperborea, where he spent the winter months.

Artemis & Boars

As well as deer, the boar (*hus*) was sacred to Artemis. As the goddess of the hunt, Artemis could also turn the hunted into the hunter, as she did when she punished King Oineus of Calydon. The King forgot to offer first fruits to Artemis when he was making sacrifices to the Gods, and she punished him by making a savage giant boar ravage his lands.

The King further angered Artemis by sending out a call for heroes to come and slay the savage Calydonian boar. After the boar was dead the King gave the meat of the boar to the heroes to eat, keeping the

[233] *Hyginus, Fabulae 172.*
[234] *Aelian, On Animals 12.4.*
[235] Vase B2365, State Hermitage Museum, St Petersburg.

head and hide as his privilege. Because of its strength and ferocity, a boar would have been considered a worthy opponent for any hunter and thus a giant boar was a great prize.

Artemis, obviously displeased at the killing of the boar, sowed discord amongst the hunters. She caused the sons of Thestio to seize the hide and in declaring that it was their share of the spoils, a war broke out between their people (the Kouretes) and the heroes of the Calydonians who had also helped in the hunt.[236]

During the hunt for the boar a prince of Arcadia called Ankaios boasted that not even Artemis would stop him from slaying it. Artemis proved him wrong by making the boar slay him with its tusks.

Another prince who offended Artemis with his boasts was Adonis, the lover of Aphrodite, from the Mediterranean island of Cyprus, who she had killed in the same manner on the tusks of a wild boar.

The tale of the founding of Ephesus recounted by Herodotus attributes the location of Ephesus to the place where a boar was killed, fulfilling the words of the oracle that *"a fish and a boar will show you the way"*.

An interesting tale recounts the dream of Phintias, ruler of Acragas, who dreamed that whilst hunting boar he was slain by a wild sow. To appease Artemis he had coins made with her head on one side and a wild boar on the reverse.[237] This must have worked, as Phintias went on to live for some years afterwards.

Artemis & Bulls

Artemis was also on occasion associated with the bull. Her title of Tauropolos indicates this, from the founding of the Taurean tribe in Skythia by Iphigeneia after a bull was substituted in her place by Artemis. It is also interesting to note that Theseus founded a temple to *Artemis Soteira* after slaying the Minotaur.[238]

---

[236] *Antoninus Liberalis, Metamorphoses; Ovid, Metamorphoses 2.*
[237] *Diodorus Siculus 22.5.*
[238] *Pausanias 2.31.4.*

Pausanias mentions a relief in front of the temple of Apollo at Argolis, of a fight between a bull and a wolf with a maiden thought to be Artemis throwing a rock at the bull.[239]

There are a number of different ancient Greek coins showing Artemis riding bulls, or with Artemis on the front and a bull on the reverse. There were even bronze coins showing Artemis riding on the back of a leaping bull, with a lunar crescent beneath.[240]

Artemis & Deer

Artemis was often depicted with deer or stags, both in statues and in images on reliefs. She was Elaphobolos, *hunter of deer*, though they could find sanctuary at her temples and shrines, and she would punish hunters who tried to kill pregnant deer.

Hera referred to Artemis' love of hunting deer when she hit her, telling her she would be better off hunting deer than fighting her superiors.[241] This was perhaps unkind, as Artemis transformed herself into a deer to escape the Aloadai giants and caused them to kill each other, saving herself and Hera from their unwanted attentions.[242] Artemis also replaced Iphigeneia with a deer when she saved her from being sacrificed.

Four golden hinds pulled Artemis' chariot. The fifth was captured by Herakles (Hercules) as one of his labours, the capture of the Ceritynean Hind.[243] He wounded the hind, and had to do some smooth talking to Artemis to save himself from her wrath.[244]

As Elaphiaia means *of the deer* it is not surprising that the symbol of the deer-drawn chariot was used in her rites, to honour her. At her

[239] *Pausanias 2.19.7.*
[240] *Zeus: A Study in Ancient Religion* – Arthur Cook, volume 1:538, 1914.
[241] *Illiad 21.470*, see also *Dionysiaca 44.198.*
[242] *Apollodorus 1.53.*
[243] *Callimachus, Hymn 3 to Artemis.*
[244] *Apollodorus 2.81.*

festival at Patrai the priestess would ride on a chariot drawn by deer in honour of Artemis.[245]

The Elaphebolos festival honouring *Artemis Elaphiaia* included the making of elaphos, cakes in the shape of deer or stags, as offerings to Artemis.

Gold coins from the early 4th century BCE have been found which depicted Artemis riding on the back of a stag.[246] Along with the bull, the stag was the other main animal Artemis was shown riding on coins.

Artemis & Dogs

Dogs are one of Artemis' best known sacred animals. Many depictions of Artemis show her with a dog at her side and sometimes with her beloved hunting pack surrounding her.

The shepherd god Pan bestowed a gift of the finest hunting dogs to Artemis. He gave her six dogs - two black and white dogs, three red ones and one spotted. He also gave her seven Kynosourian bitches, famed for their tracking and hunting skills.[247] It is interesting to note the total of thirteen hounds, as it is a lunar number and dogs have a long association with the moon.

In ancient Greece dogs were bred for hunting purposes and were an expensive investment. It was believed that Artemis was responsible for the well being of all these hunting dogs.

Artemis & Fish

There were references to many of Artemis' shrines having sacred springs, and she was also associated with lakes, through temples to Artemis Limnaia (*Lady of the Lake*) which were erected on the shores

---

[245] *Pausanias 7.18.8*

[246] *Greek Coins* – Charles Seltman, p181, 1933.

[247] *Callimachus, Hymn 3 to Artemis.*

of lakes. As a result of this fresh-water fish were considered to be sacred to her, presumably as a different type of prey.[248]

The nymphs of Syrakouse[249] were said to have caused a great fountain to gush forth to please Artemis, which contained fish in huge numbers that were held sacred to Artemis and taboo, it being forbidden to remove them.[250]

There was also a sacred spring at Syrakouse, which was the nymph Arethousa after she had been transformed to save her from rape. This spring was said to contain a tame sacred eel.[251]

A fish figured in the founding of the city of Ephesus where the largest and most famous temple of Artemis was located. The oracle had said *"a fish and a boar will show you the way"*, and it was whilst the men were making a fire to cook the fish they had caught that a boar was scared from the bushes and subsequently killed, providing the location at its death spot for the city.

Artemis & Hares

The hare is associated with Artemis through the foundation myth of the colony of Boiai. When they consulted an oracle, the settlers were told that the goddess would show them where to dwell, and then a hare appeared, guided the settlers to the spot, and disappeared into a myrtle tree.[252]

In Aeschylus' *Agamemnon* the goddess was said to demand the sacrifice of Iphigeneia because she was angry that a pregnant hare was killed by an eagle near the palace of Agamemnon. This was also said to be an omen for the destruction of Troy, with the hare representing Troy and the eagle the avenging Greeks.

---

[248] *Diodorus Siculus 5.2.3.*
[249] Modern day Sicily
[250] *Diodorus Siculus 5.2.3-5.5.1.*
[251] *Aelian, On Animals 8.4.*
[252] *Pausanias 3.22.12.*

Artemis, Lions & Leopards

Both the lion and leopard were frequently depicted in association with Artemis. At Ephesus, one of her primary temples, we find depictions of lions.[253] Pausanias describes Artemis holding a lion in her left hand and a leopard in her right,[254] which may refer to images of Artemis such as that on an 8th century BCE vase found in Italy.

This is also suggestive of the gods who were most important to Artemis – the lion as a symbol of Apollo and the leopard as a symbol of Dionysus.

In the *Illiad*, Artemis was called a *"lion among women"*, further emphasizing the leonine connection.[255] Theocritus too, uses leonine symbolism, describing the beasts going to the grove of Artemis, and in the centre a lioness, comparing Artemis to the lioness.[256]

> *"The Child of Zeus, the tireless Huntress Artemis sleeping, what time her feet forwearied are with following lions with her flying shafts over the hills far-stretching."*[257]

Artemis is depicted hunting some sort of large feline on a 7th century BCE Corinthian vase. It is not clear whether this is a lion or a leopard, but this does demonstrate that the whole big cat motif was evident from an early period. As a solar beast we might expect to see the lion more connected with Apollo, but this was not the case until centuries later, reinforcing the strength of the Artemis-lion connection.

Although the leopard was traditionally sacred to Dionysus, we may also note that it was seen frequently in company with Artemis. The temple of Artemis at Corfu had a central winged figure flanked by two leopards over the entrance. This figure is often described as a Gorgo (hideous apotropaic figure akin to a Sheela-na-gig) and may have been a masked figure of Artemis herself. The use of grotesque

---

[253] *The Earlier Temple of Artemis at Ephesus* – W.R. Lethaby, *Journal of Hellenic Studies*, 1917 1:1-16.
[254] *Pausanias 5.19.5.*
[255] *Illiad 21.470.*
[256] *Theocritus, Theocritus.*
[257] *Quintus Smyrnaeus, Fall of Troy 1.905.*

Artemis and the Big Cats
*Based on the image of Artemis Potnia on an 8th century BCE vase found in Italy,
this image shows the goddess holding a large feline in each hand. The image also
clearly shows Artemis as a winged goddess.*

initiation masks in ceremonies has been suggested from masks found at the sanctuary of *Artemis Orthia* in Sparta.[258]

An 8th century BCE vase from Italy showed Artemis as Queen of the Beasts with a leopard in one hand and stag in the other.[259] A 5th century BCE vase shows Artemis wearing a leopard-skin cloak, feeding a swan.[260] A leopard cub is depicted on a 5th century BCE vase that shows Artemis with her brother Apollo and mother Leto.[261] The association of the leopard with Artemis (the ultimate huntress) may be due to it being such an effective hunter.

Artemis & Serpents

The twin serpents motif is also seen in association with Artemis, on coins and at temples in friezes and statues.

A coin from Aureliopos in Lydia shows Artemis with a crescent moon on her head in a chariot drawn by two snakes (2nd century BCE).[262] The Gorgo figure at Corfu also has twin serpents at her waist, rearing to face each other, repeating the motif of twin serpents.

Pausanias describes a statue of the goddess in the temple of Artemis at Despoine in Arcadia. The statue is described as a bronze image of her bearing a torch in one hand and two serpents in the other.[263]

Another serpent reference is found in Apollodorus, recounting how Artemis punished Admetos for neglecting her.

> *"While making his matrimonial sacrifices, Admetos forget to include one for Artemis. Consequently, when he opened the*

---

[258] See *The Sanctuary of Artemis Orthia at Sparta* – R.D. Dawkins, in *Journal of Hellenic Studies 5*, 1929.
[259] Vase 4209, Museo Archeologico Nazionale, Florence.
[260] Vase B2365, State Hermitage Museum, St Petersburg.
[261] Vase E256, British Museum, London.
[262] Zeus 1:245.
[263] *Pausanias 8.37.1.*

door to the bridal chamber, he found it full of the coils of serpents. Apollo told him how to propitiate the goddess.[264]

Artemis & Wolves

The wolf is the sacred animal of Apollo, but as an effective hunter it was also sacred to Artemis, as *Artemis Lykeií* which translates as *of the wolves*. This is reinforced in a late text by the Roman writer Oppian, who categorised wolves into five types – the Archer (large and tawny), the Falcon (large and silvery), the Golden Wolf (very large), the Kite (small and silvery) and an unnamed class (small and dark).[265]

That a type of wolf should be called Archer strongly hints at a connection to Artemis, as does the Golden wolf considering the number of titles she had with the word "golden" in.

Also wolves were sacred to her mother Leto after they harboured her when she was pregnant with Artemis and Apollo. From this we can see that it is likely that the wolf should be associated with Artemis as well.

---

[264] *Apollodorus 1.105.*
[265] *Oppian, Cynergetica 3:300-301 (212 CE).*

10. Goddess of the Dance & Song

"I am your servant, Artemis.
You draw your long bow at night,
clothed in the skins of wild beasts.
Now hear our beautiful singing."[266]

Artemis had a strong association with dance and song. This is emphasised by frequent references in Callimachus and the *Homeric Hymns*.

In the *Homeric Hymns* reference is made to Artemis leading the dances of the Muses and Graces in Apollo's house whilst they all sang.[267] Artemis is not only the leader of the dance but also the *choregos*, or leader of the choir.

Choral singing was frequently performed with the participants standing in a circle, hence the reference in Callimachus to the nymphs encircling Artemis in the dance.[268] Similarly the chorus in Euripides' *Trojan Women* refers to dancing around the temple of Artemis to honour her.[269]

In the Illiad we find the following passage, which also illustrates that dancing and singing in honour of Artemis was performed together:
"He watched her with his eyes among the girls dancing in the choir for Artemis Khryselakatos Keladeine."[270]

The choregos would stand in the centre of the circle, and be distinguished by her beauty. We see the comparison of the princess Nausicaa to Artemis when she stands amongst her attendants as choregos,[271] and find reference in the *Ephesiaca* to the beautiful maiden Antheia, who directs the other maidens and is mistaken for

---

[266] Alkman of Sparta, *c. 625 BCE.*
[267] *Homeric Hymn 27 to Artemis.*
[268] *Callimachus, Hymn 3 to Artemis.*
[269] *Euripides, Trojan Women, 551.*
[270] *Illiad 16.181.*
[271] *Odyssey 6.151.*

Artemis by the crowds because of her outstanding beauty and height.[272]

A recent work on ancient Greek dance observes that Artemis as the choregos was consistent with the Delian ritual performance of hymns, as referred to in works like Euripides' *Hecuba*.[273]

One of the oldest choral songs known is from 7th century BCE Sparta, by the poet Alkman. It is entitled *A Hymn to Artemis of the Strict Observance*, and described as being for a chorus of Spartan girls dressed as doves to sing at dawn on the Feast of the Plough. The reference to doves may well indicate the girls should be dressed as nymphs, as the word *doves* is a translation of Pleiades, the seven nymph sisters who were companions of Artemis for a while.

A form of choral song that must be considered is the paean, which was distinct from the choral hymns. Paeans were songs of gratitude or propitiation originally sung to Artemis or Apollo. Originally these were sung by young men with young women supplying the ritual cries, but they were subsequently also performed by choruses of young women.

Euripides describes Iphigeneia asking a chorus of girls from Chalcis to sing a propitiating paean to Artemis whilst moving round her temple and altar.[274] Sophocles also refers to young girls singing a paean to Artemis and her nymphs.[275]

The *Homeric Hymn to Aphrodite* also made reference to Artemis loving dancing, the lyre and strong-voiced song.[276] The *Homeric Hymn to Pythian Apollo*[277] mentions *Artemis Iokheaira* singing with the Muses.

Whilst singing is mentioned occasionally, dance seems to have been more significant. It is quite likely that dances played an important part in some of the ceremonies of Artemis. It was said of her, *"Where has*

---

[272] *Xenophon, Ephesiaca.*
[273] *Dance and Ritual Play in Greek Religion* – Stephen Lonsdale, p66.
[274] *Euripides, Iphigeneia at Aulis, 1467, 1480.*
[275] *Sophocles, Trojan Women.*
[276] *Homeric Hymn 5 to Aphrodite.*
[277] *Homeric Hymn 3 to Apollo.*

not Artemis danced?"[278] We see her given titles such as *Kordax* (of
the Cordax, a dance from Lydia) and in the Greek Magical Papyri she
is called *"O song and dance".*[279]

Callimachus refers to Artemis several times in association with dance,
saying: *"[Artemis] whose study is the bow ... and the spacious dance"*,
and *"when the Nymphs encircle thee in the dance"*, going on to
remark that the sun god Helios paused to watch her dance in the mid-
summer, causing the day to lengthen.[280]

Thus it is not surprising that her maidens danced at Ephesus, or that
young girls had to "dance the she-bear" at Brauron. At the Temple of
Ephesus the maidens were described to, *"sport and lightly leap and
clap their hands in the temple of Artemis the Fair at Ephesos, now
sinking down upon their haunches and again springing up, like the
hopping wagtail."*[281]

Pausanias mentions the annual dancing and choral singing at Karyai
in Lacedaimonia around an image of Artemis that was set out in the
open.[282] The dance performed by the maidens was known as the
Karyatis, and was described as a spirited jig, with many pirouettes and
whirls.

The Cordax is the subject of much debate. It is known that this dance
was sacred to Artemis,[283] but it has been suggested that it was either
a circle dance, or a sinuous serpentine type dance without moving the
feet. A gloss by Hesychius refers to Spartan women dancers called
korythalistriai who danced at a festival for *Artemis Korythalia*.

Weapon dances are represented in Greek art from as early as the
eighth century BCE, and were particularly disseminated from Crete
and Sparta. The dancers of such dances were known as pyrrhichists.
The most widely represented group of pyrrhichists is female.[284]

---

[278] *Proverbia Aesopi No 9, p229.*
[279] *PGM VII:686-702.*
[280] *Callimachus, Hymn 3 to Artemis.*
[281] *Aelian, On Animals 12.9.*
[282] *Pausanias 3.10.7.*
[283] *Pausanias 6.22.1.*
[284] *Dance and Ritual Play in Greek Religion* – Stephen Lonsdale, p144.

Pyrrichists performed nude with helmet and greaves, and a shield and weapon such as sword, spear or javelin.

The origins of the war dances are hinted at by Callimachus who said: *"the Amazons ... and Hippo [their Queen] performed a holy rite for thee, and they .... around the image danced a war-dance - first in shields and armour, and again in a circle arraying a spacious choir."*[285] This would also fit with the Amazons being said to have founded the town of Pyrrhikhos in Lacedaimonia The term pyrrichist may well be derived from Pyrrhikhos.

An Attic vase from around 440 BCE shows Artemis carrying her bow and a long torch with a dancing male pyrrichist in front of her.[286]Hippo, Queen of the Amazons, was turned into a horse by Artemis for refusing to perform the annual dance around the altar at Ephesus.[287]

In the *Homeric Hymn 5 to Aphrodite*, whilst denying that she was a goddess to persuade a young man into her bed, Aphrodite describes herself being abducted from the dance of the huntress Artemis, of the golden arrows.[288] This theme of abduction of the dancing maidens from an Artemis temple or ceremony was a common one.

Herodotus refers to the abduction by raiding Pelasgians of Athenian women from Brauron whilst they were celebrating the festival of Artemis there.[289] Plutarch describes the abduction of Helen by Theseus and Peirithous when she was dancing at the sanctuary of *Artemis Orthia*. Pausanias also reports the abduction of girls performing dances for *Artemis Karyae* at Sparta by the hero Aristomenes and his men.[290] When some of his men get drunk and try to rape the virgins, Aristomenes kills them, and ransoms the girls back unharmed, possibly to avoid the wrath of Artemis. We may also note that Persephone was in the company of Artemis and Athena and many nymphs when she was abducted by Hades.[291]

---

[285] *Callimachus, Hymn 3 to Artemis.*
[286] Museo Archeologico Nazionale, Naples, 81908 (H3010), cat no 6.40.
[287] *Callimachus Hymn 3 to Artemis.*
[288] *Homeric Hymn 5 to Aphrodite.*
[289] *Herodotus 6.138.*
[290] *Pausanias 4.16.9.*
[291] *Homeric Hymn 2 to Demeter, Pausanias 8.31.2.*

11. Goddess of Water

Come with bows bent and with emptying of quivers,
Maiden most perfect, lady of light,
With a noise of winds and many rivers,
With a clamour of waters, and with might;
Bind on thy sandals, O thou most fleet,
Over the splendour and speed of thy feet;
For the faint east quickens, the wan west shivers,
Round the feet of the day and the feet of the night.

Atalanta in Calydon, Algernon Charles Swinburne, 1865

Artemis has a strong association with water, as the Lady of the Lake, *Artemis Limnaia*. There were a number of shrines to Artemis with this title, and sacred springs and pools were common at Artemis temples.

She demonstrated her power over water on three occasions by turning people into springs. Artemis saw Pan chasing her nymph companion Pholoe, and transformed Pholoe into a spring to escape the god's attentions. [292]

The nymph Arethousa prayed to Artemis for help when fleeing the unwanted attentions of the river god Alpheios. Arethousa had been a loyal devotee of Artemis, so the goddess transformed Arethousa into a spring and took her to the precinct of her shrine on the island of Syrakouse (near Sicily). This spring contained a tame sacred eel that accepted food.[293]

Subsequently the priests of *Artemis Soteira* at Aegium performed a ritual of throwing offering cakes into the sea, saying that they were sending them to Arethousa in Syrakouse. The implication is that Artemis would ensure the cakes travelled across the waters of the sea to the spring at Syrakouse.[294]

---

[292] *Silvae 2.3.1*
[293] *Aelian, On Animals 8.4.*
[294] *Pausanias 7.24.3.*

Peirene, another nymph, from Corinthos in Southern Greece, was also turned into a spring by Artemis. Artemis had accidentally killed Peirene's son and the nymph was inconsolable. So Artemis, feeling sorry for Peirene, transformed her into a fountain-spring so she could weep eternally.[295]

Zeus also made Artemis the goddess of roads and harbours, tying her in as a goddess of the ways. Callimachus described her as the *"Watcher over roads and harbors."*[296]

In the *Argonautica* Artemis is described as *"saviour of ships"* when a song is sung in her honour.[297]

[295] *Pausanias 2.3.2.*
[296] *Callimachus, Hymn 3 to Artemis.*
[297] *Argonautica 2.570.*

12. Warrior Goddess

A number of instances are recorded of thanks being given to Artemis for her participation in battle, or support ensuring victory. Thus the Greeks honoured her for her participation in the battle of Artemision, and the Athenians annually sacrificed goats to her for the victory at Marathon.

Xenophon described long lines of soldiers marching from the gymnasiums to dedicate their wreaths to Artemis in Ephesus.[298] Strabo describes carvings on the pillar of the temple at Amarynthos showing the Artemis festival procession containing three thousand soldiers, six hundred horsemen and sixty chariots, emphasisng her martial connection.[299]

Artemis herself was not averse to fighting in battle, as was shown by her participation in the Indian Wars of Dionysus, and in the defence of Olympus against the giants, when she slew the giant Aigaion with her arrows.[300]

Artemis was one of the patrons of the Amazons, along with the war god Ares. The Amazons were reputed to have founded several of the famous shrines to Artemis, including the major temple at Ephesus[301] and the temple at Pyrrhikhos in Lacedaimonia.[302]

Artemis was particularly honoured at Sparta, the most martial of Greek cities. There were temples to her as *Artemis Diktynna*, *Artemis Aiginaií*, *Artemis Issoria*, *Artemis Hígemoní* , *Artemis Knagia*, *Artemis Korythalia* and the most significant, *Artemis Orthia*.

The temple of Artemis at Euboia had an inscription on one of the pillars honouring the nearby battle that had occurred:

---

[298] *Xenophon, Agesilaus.*
[299] *Strabo 10.1.10.*
[300] *Apollodorus 1.38.*
[301] *Pausanias 7.2.6.*
[302] *Pausanias 3.25.3.*

With numerous tribes from Asia's regions brought
The sons of Athens on these waters, fought;
Erecting, after they had quelled the Mede,
To Artemis this record of the deed.[303]

Weapon dances were also associated with Artemis, as shown in an Attic vase from around 440 BCE, which shows Artemis carrying her bow and a long torch with a dancing male pyrrichist in front of her.[304]

The war dances may well have begun with the Amazons, as hinted at by Callimachus.[305] The Amazons worshiped Artemis as one of their tutelary deities along with Ares.

---

[303] *Plutarch, Lives.*
[304] Museo Archeologico Nazionale, Naples, 81908 (H3010), cat no 6.40.
[305] *Callimachus, Hymn 3 to Artemis.*

13. The Revenge of Artemis

Artemis frequently displayed a wrathful side to her nature. In many instances there was a justified reason for this and parallels can be drawn between Artemis and the goddess Nemesis, as both are seen dispensing divine vengeance.

In his *Hymn 3 to Artemis*, Callimachus summarises the actions that incur her wrath. These include dishonouring her altar, disputing her supremacy as an archer or huntress, attempting to woo her, or not attending her annual dance.[306]

Artemis was also very protective of her mother Leto and would with her twin brother Apollo, take revenge on all those who turned her mother away when she was pregnant. Again it is with her brother that she revenges her mother's pride against the harsh words spoken by Queen Niobe killing her children and against the giant Tityos who tries to force himself on Leto. These incidents clearly illustrates the importance that Artemis placed on family relationships.

As a fierce and wrathful goddess, Artemis could also be appealed to for protection.

> *"Artemis ... give ear to my prayers and ward off the evil Keres [Death-Spirits]. For you, goddess, this is no small thing, but for me it is critical."*[307]

> *"Philerátis dedicated this image to Artemis. Accept it, Lady, and watch over her safety."*[308]

Actaeon

Actaeon (or Aktaion) was a prince of Thebes and keen hunter, who had the misfortune of seeing Artemis naked as she bathed in a

---

[306] *Callimachus, Hymn 3 to Artemis.*
[307] *Theognis 1.11.*
[308] *Callimachus, Epigram 31.*

stream. In her fury Artemis transformed him into a stag, and he was slain by his own hounds.[309]

A nymph spotted Actaeon hiding in his tree and screamed, alerting Artemis, who slid under the water to cover herself. Artemis made his dogs kill him slowly whilst he retained his human awareness, as punishment for seeking to see her naked.[310]

The Death of Actaeon
This image, based on a depiction on a 450 BCE vase, shows Actaeon being attacked by his hounds. Many similar depictions have been found and this myth also inspired many artists, notably Cesari and Titian who painted scenes from it.

---

[309] *Hyginus Fabulae 181; Ovid, Metamorphoses 3.138; Apollodorus, The Library 3.30, Callimachus Hymn 5.106, The Bath of Pallas.*
[310] *Dionysiaca 5.305-336.*

Adonis

Adonis, the Cyprian prince and lover of Aphrodite, offended Artemis by saying that he was a better hunter than the goddess. She responded by sending a boar to gore and kill him.[311] This was a contributory factor to the ongoing feud between Aphrodite and Artemis.

Aristomelidas

Artemis stirred up the hero Khronios to slay king Aristomelidas after he had defiled a maiden, making Khronis the strong arm of her vengeance. After killing the King, Khronis fled to Tegea and set up a sanctuary to Artemis, displaying unusually good sense for a hero.[312]

Bouphagos

Artemis was famous for her chastity, which some foolish mortals took as a challenge. The inevitable consequence of trying to molest Artemis was death, as shown in the tale of Bouphagos, who attempted to rape her and was killed for his sacrilege.[313]

Hippo

The Amazonian Queen Hippo, who with her fellow Amazons was said to have founded the shrine of Artemis at Ephesus, refused to dance around the altar. In her anger Artemis transformed Hippo into her namesake - a horse.[314]

---

[311] *Apollodorus 3.183.*
[312] *Pausanias 8.47.6.*
[313] *Pausanias 8.27.17.*
[314] *Callimachus, Hymn 3 to Artemis.*

Koronis

Koronis was a Princess of Trikka in Thessalia who was beloved of Apollo. She slept with another man during her pregnancy by Apollo, and Artemis killed her during the labour with her arrows for the insult to her brother. A different version of the myth has Artemis killing Koronis as a reprisal for Apollo's subterfuge in causing the death of Orion.

Artemis also killed many of Koronis' neighbours as well for not keeping a better eye on her.[315] Hermes snatched her child from the flames to save it when the body of Koronis was being burned on a funeral pyre.[316]

Leimon

Artemis and Apollo never forgot that their mother Leto had been turned away in every land she visited when she was pregnant with them. Only the island of Delos, which became a cult centre of worship for Artemis, took the pregnant Leto in. As a consequence of this the divine twins took it upon themselves to make many people suffer.

Whilst the Prince Skephros was apologizing to Apollo, his brother Prince Leimon came rushing in and killed him, in fear that he was being accused. Artemis immediately slew Leimon in vengeance.[317]

Lomaitho and Melanippos

The biggest sacrilege that could be done to Artemis was to defile the sanctity of her temple. This was done by one of her priestesses Lomaitho, who made love with her lover Melanippos in the temple, in the inner sanctuary of Artemis at Patrai.

---

[315] *Pindar, Pythian 3.*
[316] *Pausanias 2.26.6.*
[317] *Pausanias 8.53.1.*

The wrath of the goddess for this insult was inflicted on all around. The earth yielded no harvests, and strange and fatal diseases began to afflict the population. When the people went to the Delphic Oracle the Pythian priestess accused the lovers and ordered their sacrifice to Artemis. Additionally the fairest maiden and youth were to be sacrificed each year. From these sacrifices the river flowing by the sanctuary gained its name of Ameilikhos (*Relentless*).[318]

The Daughters of Niobe

At the request of her mother Leto, Artemis killed six of the seven daughters of Quuen Niobe, as punishment for her boasting to be more blessed than Leto due to her large number of children (seven sons and seven daughters).[319] For more detail of this see the section on *Queen Niobe of Thebes* in chapter 5 *Artemis in the Myths*.

Python

The Python was a giant serpent or dragon that guarded the shrine of Delphi. During her pregnancy, Leto was pursued across the lands by the Python. After their birth, Apollo and Artemis killed the Python with their arrows (some versions attribute this slaying to Apollo only). Apollo subsequently took over the shrine at Delphi and it became sacred to him.

Following on from the killing of the Python, Artemis and Apollo then punished the Corinthians for turning them away when they had come seeking purification for the killing of the ancient beast. The Delphic Oracle, previous home of the Python, became a place of ritual purification under Apollo, ensuring the need to rely on any other place for purification was removed.

If Artemis was angered, she would not hesitate to strike down the wrong-doer with her arrows or with disease or sudden death.

---

[318] *Pausanias 7.19.1.*
[319] *Apollodorus, The Library 3.46.*

> *"Artemis Khrysenios killed Ladomeia the daughter of Bellerophontes in anger."*[320]

Artemis was always ready to slay humans who had offended the gods she cared most about, especially her mother Leto, her brother Apollo and her hunting partner Dionysus.

> *"Tityos saw Leto when she came to Pytho and in a fit of passion tried to embrace her. But she called out to her children [Artemis & Apollo], who shot him dead with arrows. He is being punished even in death, for vultures feast on his heart in Hades' realm."*[321]

As a god of the wilds who was worshipped mainly by women it makes sense that Dionysus would be friends with Artemis. Neither spent much time away from the wilds, and both enjoyed hunting and dance. One version of the tale of Ariadne has her slain by Artemis for betraying Dionysus.[322]
Artemis frequently sent disease to punish those who had offended her. In this respect she is similar to the Egyptian lioness goddess Sekhmet, who through her seven arrows could either heal or send disease.

> *And both pestilential diseases and sudden deaths are imputed to these gods [Artemis and Apollo].*[323]

---

[320] *Illiad 6.205.*
[321] *Apollodorus 1.22.*
[322] *Odyssey 11.324.*
[323] *Strabo 14.1.6.*

14. Goddess of the Sun & Moon

Today Artemis is populary viewed as a lunar goddess and in particular with the New Moon when the moon is said to resemble the hunting bow of Artemis. Evidence for this association with the moon can be found in classical literature, showing that indeed Artemis has been viewed as a lunar goddess since ancient times.

Examples of this can be found in *Hymn 3* of Callimachus when he wrote: *"And how often goddess, didst thou make trial of thy silver bow?"*[324] We also find a passage in *The Contest of Homer and Hesiod* which refers to her bow as being silver: *"[Artemis] slew Callisto with a shot of her silver bow."*[325]

Classical literature does however also provide us with evidence showing that her bow was considered to be of gold or as being gold in colour. The *Homeric Hymn 27 to Artemis* refers to her golden bow, saying of her, *"Over the shadowy hills and windy peaks she draws her golden bow."*

Ovid also makes reference to the golden bow, writing in his *Metamorphoses*, *"Syrinx revered Ortygia [Artemis]; girt like her she well might seem, so easy to mistake … were not her bow of horn, Latonia's gold."*[326]

From this it should be clear that the colour of her bow alone does not provide enough evidence to classify Artemis as a goddess of the moon.

Later images of the goddess also shows her with a lunar crescent on her head, reinforcing her associations with the moon, especially during the Roman era, when she became synomous with Diana, the Roman goddess of the moon.

Artemis also assumes many of the powers and associations of the Greek goddess of the moon, Selene, which provides further reasons

---

[324] *Callimachus, Hymn 3 to Artemis.*
[325] *Of the Origins of Homer and Hesiod, And of Their Contest 316.*
[326] *Ovid, Metamorphoses, 1.693.*

for considering her a lunar goddess. This may well be due to the Titan nature of Selene, as she and Helios were largely replaced by Artemis and Apollo, Olympians of the reigning order.

The Greek Lyric fragments give further associations with the moon, when they recount that Artemis was said to give particularly easy childbirth at the full moon to people and animals.[327] These full moon references hint at Artemis-Selene, as Selene was particularly associated with the full moon.

Solid evidence for Artemis being a lunar goddess is found in the 2nd century BCE with the Stoics, in Apollodorus *Stoic 40* and Diogenes *Bab Diels Doxogr 549 b7* where the association is made clear. By the time of Plutarch (*Quaest Conv 659*) in the 1st to 2nd century CE, it is taken as read that Artemis is a lunar goddess.

In the *Dionysiaca*, the shade of the dying Actaeon describes Artemis to his father as being like *"the full moon of evening flashing through the water"*.[328]

Although references to Artemis as being a moon goddess are not as frequent as one would expect, it could be that it was so well known, that there was no reason for writers of the time to make mention of it.

However looking at the myths and titles of Artemis we also find many references and a great deal of symbolism which provide us with a clear argument that she was also a goddess of the sun, or which at the very least are ambigious to the point that it is difficult to distinguish one over the other.

An example of this is when Artemis speaks to her father Zeus and asks him to *"give me to be Phaesphoria [Bringer of Light]"*.[329] This could be a reference to either the sun or moon.

A quote from the *Dionysiaca* could suggest a lunar or solar radiance from her face, describing her as *"diffusing radiance from her face"*,[330] and she was also known as the *"fair-faced Bringer of Light."*[331]

---

[327] *Greek Lyric I Alcaeus Frag 390 (from Scholiast on Illiad).*
[328] *Dionysiaca 5.485*
[329] *Callimachus, Hymn 3 to Artemis.*

The reference by Athenaios that amphiphontes were offered at temples of Artemis and at crossroads when the sky was lit by both the sun and the moon from either side suggests a joining of both sun and moon in the celebration of Artemis.[332]

A further argument for Artemis as a goddess of the sun can be made through the numerous references found between Artemis and the colour and the metal gold, which has long been associated with the sun. In fact, gold has been perceived as the metal of the sun since at least 3000 BCE in ancient Egypt, whose religious and social structures strongly influenced those of ancient Greece. Many of her titles and associations also make references to gold.

Artemis' Golden Chariot
Artemis drives a golden chariot, pulled by four golden hinds, once again hinting at a solar connection. It also recalls the golden chariot of the sun god Helios.

> *"[Artemis] swiftly drives her all-golden chariot..*"[333]

Indeed the golden motif is carried to an extreme in the *Hymn 3 to Artemis* by Callimachus in the 3rd century BCE, in a very solar reference.

> *"Artemis, Virgin, Slayer of Tityos, golden were your arms and golden your belt, you yoked a golden chariot, and golden bridles, you put on your deer."*[334]

Artemis' Golden Reins
The golden tracery of her chariot probably led to the title of Khrysenios, (*of the golden reins*), found in the *Illiad*.[335] This title is also used for Ares in the *Odyssey*.

---

[330] *Dionysiaca 48.302.*
[331] *Callimachus, Hymn 3 to Artemis 188.*
[332] *Athenaios, Deipnosophistai 14.645a.*
[333] *Homeric Hymn 9 to Artemis.*
[334] *Callimachus, Hymn 3 to Artemis.*
[335] *Illiad 6.205.*

Artemis' Golden Arrows
The tile Khryselakatos means *delighting in arrows with shafts of gold*. We see this title in the *Illiad*,[336] *Homeric Hymn 27 to Artemis* and *Homeric Hymn 5 to Aphrodite*, as early references, though it does not seem to recur in later times.

Artemis of the Golden Throne
The title Khrysothronos (*golden-throned*) occurs in the *Illiad*[337] and the *Odyssey*.[338]

Artemis' Golden Sword
Herodotus uses the epithet Khrysaoros (*golden-sworded*)[339] for Artemis when describing the words of an oracle predicting the outcome of the Persian Wars.[340]

Artemis' Golden Snood
In Sophocles *Oedipus the King*, Artemis is described as having *"golden-snooded hair"*.[341] Again gold is emphasised in regard to her apparel, this time to her snood, which was a headband worn by unmarried women.

Apart from Callimachus, all of these sources are from the 9th-5th century BCE, i.e. the earlier period where there is less evidence for lunar attributions. Conversely as the lunar associations come more into evidence, there is an absence of the titles which may suggest a solar association. This may indicate a change in qualities of association and the way the goddess was perceived.

In Sophocles *Oedipus the King* reference is made to *"winged with fire, the rays of Artemis, with which, on Lycian hills, she moveth on her course"*.[342]

---

[336] *Illiad 16.181.*
[337] *Illiad 9.530.*
[338] *Odyssey 5.119.*
[339] See e.g. *Homeric Hymn 27 to Artemis.*
[340] *Herodotus 8.77.*
[341] *Sophocles, Oedipus the King, 211.*
[342] *Sophocles, Oedipus the King 216-19.*

Even more blatant than this is her title of Aithopia (*burning faced one*), which seems to directly describe the solar radiance.

A reference in Callimachus also refers to the *"unquenchable light of fire"*. What else could this refer to but the sun, the unquenchable fire in the sky?

> *"And where did you cut the pine for torches, lit by what flame? It was on Mysian Olympus, you breathed into the torches the unquenchable light of fire,"*[343]

Artemis is also associated with the lion and the leopard, both of which have long been considered to be solar creatures. In some depictions she is even shown wearing a leopard-skin cloak,[344] and is described gripping a leopard in her right hand and a lion in her left.[345]

This is a common theme in early vases, *"in the seventh century (BCE) she had been shown as a Mistress of Animals, often winged, holding one or two beasts, usually lions."*[346] The lion theme is continued in the Drachms (gold coins) issued in Massilia in the 4th century BCE which had the head of Artemis on one side, and a lion on the reverse.[347] These coins, which were frequently copied, became the chief currency of Southern Gaul at this time.

Artemis is also referred to by the title of Phoebe (Light). In this she matches her brother Apollo, who is Phoebus. If we consider Apollo for a second, he is often considered a solar god, yet he also bears the silver bow, suggesting the moon. The solar lion, associated with Artemis from a very early period, only later becomes associated with Apollo, around the fourth century BCE.

Many of the references to Artemis in association with her golden bow, fiery rays and golden items come from earlier texts from before the 5th century BCE.

---

[343] *Callimachus, Hymn 3 to Artemis.*
[344] Vase B2365, State Hermitage Museum, St Petersburg.
[345] *Pausanias 5.19.5.*
[346] *Athenian Black Figure Vases* – John Boardman, p219, 1974.
[347] *Greek Coins* – Charles Seltman, p196, 1933.

Artemis and Apollo share many qualities in their attributions, and are extremely close. So it may well be more accurate to consider the twin gods of Artemis and Apollo as being both solar, and also both lunar.

15. Relationships with the Gods

Artemis has many relationships with other deities. These relationships have a variety of forms, and include familial relationships, friendships, and identification and confusion with other goddesses.

The familial relationships are with her immediate kin, i.e. her father Zeus, her mother Leto, her twin brother Apollo and her cousin Hekate. The closest friendships include that with Dionysus, and also those with the other maiden goddesses Athena and Persephone, and Nemesis.

Artemis also had hostile relationships with other Greek deities, which seem to have been in the form of feuds over periods of time. These include her relationships with the goddesses Hera and Aphrodite.

Throughout the Greek myths and magickal papyri Artemis was at times identified or confused with a number of other goddesses as being the same goddess. This range of goddesses spreads across more than one pantheon. In the Greek pantheon she was identified with the moon goddess Selene and the liminal goddess Hekate.

She was also identified with the Cretan hunting goddess Britomartis or Dictynna (Diktynna), who were described as being either separate companions or as titles of Artemis.

Artemis was identified at times with the Egyptian cat goddess Bastet, the Roman lunar goddess Diana and the Thracian goddess Bendis.

Artemis & Aphrodite

There was antipathy between these two goddesses. Artemis was one of the three goddesses unaffected by Aphrodite's power, along with Athena and Hestia. This angered Aphrodite, as the young women (or men) who dedicated themselves to Artemis were often the most beautiful, like Atalanta and Hippolytus.

Prince Hippolytus, a favourite of Artemis, was slain through the wiles of Aphrodite.[348] This rivalry is shown in detail in Euripides' *Hippolytus*, where Aphrodite through her wiles has Hippolytus killed for spurning love and devoting himself to Artemis and a life of celibacy and hunting. In revenge Artemis sent the boar which wounded and killed Adonis, Aphrodite's lover.[349]

Aphrodite was also responsible for the loss through rape, death or marriage of several of the companions of Artemis, including Syrinx, Polyphonte and Atalanta.

Artemis & Apollo

As twins, Artemis and Apollo were very close. Their bond begins at birth, with Artemis assisting in the birth of Apollo shortly after her own birth. The two were usually shown seated together in images of Olympus. Callimachus said that although all the gods bade her sit next to them, Artemis always sat next to Apollo.[350]

Together the twins were very protective of their mother Leto, killing the Python which had chased her and many people who had refused her shelter when she was pregnant with them. They also slew the giant Tityos for trying to molest Leto, and the children of Queen Niobe after she boasted she was more blessed than Leto and offended her.

For twins who were close, it is unsurprising to see they shared roles and titles, such as both being protectors of children (Artemis the girls and Apollo the boys), and being known as Phoebe and Phoebus. Both also shared the ability to send pestilence and sudden death.[351]

The festival of Thargelia (First Fruits) celebrated their birth on the 6th and 7th Thargelion. Together Apollo and Artemis were patrons of the Hyperboreoi.

---

[348] *Pausanias 2.27.4.*
[349] *Apollodorus 3.183.*
[350] *Callimachus, Hymn 3 to Artemis.*
[351] *Strabo 14.1.6.*

Artemis & Ares

The main connecting factor between Artemis and Ares is the fact that they were the patron deities of the Amazons. Artemis and Ares were both honoured at her shrine on the Ilissos in Athens as *Artemis Agrotera* and *Ares Enyalios*, and honoured at the festival of Charisteria, which celebrated the victory over the Persians at the battle of Marathon; an unusual occurrence as she was more often celebrated with Apollo.

Hyginus recorded that the mythical Amazon queen Otrera, a wife of Ares, was the founder of the temple of Artemis at Ephesus.[352] It is also interesting to observe that Ares was said to have provided a flock of birds which shot arrows from their feathers to guard the island sanctuary of the Amazons.[353] Birds that fire arrows immediately bring Artemis, the other tutelary deity of the Amazons, to mind.

Another connection between these two deities is the pyrrichists (war-dancers), who danced in war gear with weapons, linking the god of war (Ares) with the goddess of dance (Artemis).

Artemis & Athena & Persephone

The goddesses Athena and Persephone were raised with Artemis on the isle of Sicily, and were all virgin maidens together (until the abduction of Persephone by Hades). Together the three maidens wove Zeus' robe and gathered flowers. Because of their happy memories of this time this island was said to be the favourite of these goddesses.[354]

The three maidens were all said to have been gathering flowers with nymphs when Hades rose from the underworld in his chariot and abducted Persephone.[355]

---

[352] *Hyginus, Fabulae 223, 225*
[353] *Hyginus, Fabulae 30.*
[354] *Diodorus Siculus 5.2.3.*
[355] *Homeric Hymn 2 to Demeter.*

Artemis & Aura

Aura, the Titan goddess of the breeze was a close companion of Artemis until she offended her. She even received the honour of riding in Artemis' chariot with her.[356]

Artemis complained to the vengeance goddess Nemesis about Aura insulting her body and the size of her breasts. Nemesis replied by telling Artemis that she would see Aura in a mountain stream weeping for her lost virginity.[357]

After Dionysus had molested her in her sleep, Aura was furious and killed many people. As her pregnancy developed, Artemis taunted her, returning the jibes that Aura had directed at her. To complete her revenge, Artemis delayed her arrival when Aura was in labour, to ensure that she had as painful a childbirth as possible.

Aura gave birth to twins, one of whom she devoured. Artemis snatched the other twin away and gave him to his father Dionysus to look after. Aura, still mad, committed suicide by jumping into a river.[358]

Artemis & Bastet

The association of Artemis with Bastet is less obvious, although the Egyptians had venerated cats for centuries as hunters, killing dangerous snakes and also mice and rats to protect the grain supply.

Herodotus is the main writer on the link between Artemis and Bastet. He describes the frequent assemblies held in Boubastis, the cult-centre of Bastet's worship in Egypt in honour of Artemis, which he gives as the Greek translation of Boubastis![359]

He went on to describe the city of Bouto as the centre for a great Egyptian oracle where there was a temple of Apollo and Artemis (the

---

[356] *Dionysiaca 48.302.*
[357] *Dionysiaca 48.375.*
[358] *Dionysiaca 48.848.*
[359] *Herodotus 2.59.*

106

Egyptian deities Horus and Bastet).[360] In his writings Herodotus also identifies Dionysus with Osiris and Demeter with Isis, and says that this is where the poet Aiskhylos came up with the idea that Artemis was the daughter of Demeter.[361]

A later tale had the monster Typhon attacking the Olympian gods, who fled to Egypt and changed into animal forms to hide. Artemis assumed the form of a cat.[362]

Artemis & Bendis

The Thracian goddess Bendis was known to the Greeks by the 6th century BCE, being mentioned in a fragment by the poet Hipponax.[363] She was later called "two-speared" in the comedy *The Thracian Women* by Cratinus in 442 BCE.[364] This is significant as Artemis was sometimes depicted carrying two hunting spears.

> *"They [the Thracians] worship no gods but Ares, Dionysus, and Artemis [Ares, Sabazios and Bendis]. Their princes ... worship Hermes [Zalmoxis]."*[365]

There is little recorded information about Bendis, though Herodotus mentions Thracian and Paionian women having straw with them when they sacrificed to the Artemis Basileis (*royal*) [i.e. Bendis].[366]

Plato also mentions Artemis and Bendis as being equated in *The Republic*, saying *"Bendis, the Thracian Artemis".*[367]

---

[360] *Herodotus 2.155.*
[361] *Herodotus 2.156.*
[362] *Antoninus Liberalis, Metamorphoses 28; Ovid, Metamorphoses 5.319.*
[363] *Hipponax fragment 127 in Les fragments du poète Hiponnax – O. Masson, 1962.*
[364] *Fragment 85 in Poetae Comici Graeci – R Kassel & C. Austin, 1983.*
[365] *Herodotus 5.7.*
[366] *Herodotus 4.33.*
[367] *Plato, The Republic, Book 1.*

Artemis & Britomartis

Artemis was associated with the Cretan goddess Britomartis (meaning *sweet maiden*). Britomartis was also known as Diktynna (meaning *of the nets*), a title that was subsequently used for Artemis. By the 5th century BCE this goddess had largely become assimilated into Artemis.[368]

> *"They [the Spartans] surname her [Artemis] also Limnaie [Lady of the Lake], though she is not really Artemis but Britomartis of Crete."*[369]

Apuleius mentions Artemis describing herself as *"Dictynna Diana to the arrowbearing Cretans."*[370] This title is also used in the *Orphic Hymns*, where she was described as *"torch-bearing Goddess, Diktynna divine"*.[371]

Britomartis was said to have been born at Caino in Crete, the daughter of Zeus and Carme, making her a half-sister to Artemis. She invented the hunting nets (*diktya*) from which she took her name and was seen in earlier times as a hunting companion of Artemis.[372]

The hill on Crete from which Britomartis leapt to escape the attentions of King Minos was called Diktaion (*hill of nets*), and altars were set up there to sacrifice to her. Callimachus states that the garlands worn were pine or mastic, but never myrtle.[373]

Artemis & Dionysus

After Leto and Apollo, Dionysus seems to be the god most associated with Artemis. Artemis fights on his side in the Indian Wars of Dionysus, trying to help him when Hera sends him mad.[374]

---

[368] *Cretan Cults and Festivals* – R.F. Willetts, p183, 1962.

[369] *Pausanias 3.14.2.*

[370] *Apuleius 11.5.*

[371] *Orphic Hymn 36 to Artemis.*

[372] *Diodorus Siculus 5.76.3.*

[373] *Callimachus, Hymn 3 to Artemis.*

[374] See e.g. *Dionysiaca 32.100, 36.28.*

It is not surprising that there should have been a bond between Artemis, as a goddess of the wilds worshipped by women, and Dionysus, a god of the wilds worshipped by women. Dionysus was the half-brother of Artemis (they were both fathered by Zeus), and would on occasions hunt with Artemis.[375] Pindar describes Artemis yoking savage lions for Dionysus.[376] Dionysus was known as Bromios, and Artemis was called Bromia, also implying a connection between the two deities.

In an early version of the tale of Theseus, Artemis killed Ariadne for having been unfaithful to Dionysus at his request.[377]

As with Zeus, Artemis seems to bear Dionysus no ill will when he rapes her attendant nymphs, such as the Titan Aura, and the nymph Nikaia.

A later myth recounted by Servius describes Dionysus turning Karya, the daughter of King Dion of Laconia into a nut tree. Artemis told the Laconians what had happened and they founded the sanctuary to her there as *Artemis Karyatis*.[378]

Artemis & Hekate

> "O Artemis, Who, too, were once protectress, mighty one, Mistress, who burst forth from the earth, dog-leader, All-tamer, crossroad goddess, triple-headed, Bringer of light, august virgin, I call you Fawn-slayer, crafty, O infernal one, And many-formed."[379]

This love spell from the Greek Magical Papyri (PGM) shows how the titles and attributes of Artemis and Hekate were frequently mingled. When we look at the way Artemis and Hekate were represented we can see that in many respects images of the two goddesses show

---

[375] *Dionysiaca 44.198*
[376] *Pindar Dithyrambs: Heracles the Bold.*
[377] *Odyssey 11.324.*
[378] *Servius, ad Verg. Bucolics 8.29.*
[379] *PGM IV:2721-26.*

similarities. Both Artemis and Hekate were beautiful maidens shown at times in short-skirts and hunting boots, and both were at times accompanied by dogs and serpents, and were shown at times with two torches.

> *"O Artemis, thou maid divine, Diktynna, huntress, fair to see, O bring that keen-nosed pack of thine, and hunt through all the house with me. O Hecate, with flaming brands."*[380]

We may also observe that the maidens performing the mystery rites at Brauron, of the bear, were dressed in saffron robes. Saffron was particularly sacred to Hekate. Euripides refers to Hekate as a daughter of Leto, making an even stronger connection to Artemis.[381]

A more obscure connection between the two goddesses occurs through the name of Hekate's mother, Asteria. Apollodorus records a fragment which hints at this, through the birthplace of Artemis being Delos, which was formerly known as Asteria.[382]

From about the 5th century BCE there was a large degree of association between Artemis and Hekate, with their names even being joined as Artemis-Hekate.

With the sharing of titles as well, (such as Enodia, Propylaií, and Phosphorus) it is clear that these two goddesses became viewed as being interwoven, with Hekate even being called the "chthonian Artemis".

> *"We pray; and that Artemis-Hekate watch over the childbed of their women."*[383]

Pausanias, Hesiod and *Lyric fragment 3.215* all refer to Iphigeneia being made into Hekate by Artemis. As Iphigeneia is herself associated with Artemis, the whole connection becomes very tangled.

---

[380] *Aristophanes, Frogs 1358.*
[381] *Euripides, Phoi, 109.*
[382] *Apollodorus 1.4.*
[383] *Aiskhylos, Suppliants, 674-7*

Artemis & Hera

As the daughter of Zeus by Leto, Artemis was never going to be popular with Hera, as she was a constant reminder of her husband's infidelity.

The main interaction between Hera and Artemis occurred in the two times they fought. Both times Hera overpowered Artemis and drove her away. The first instance of this is in the Indian Wars of Dionysus, when Hera used one of Zeus' clouds as a shield from Artemis' arrows and then threw chunks of hail at her, breaking her bow and knocking her over.[384]
Towards the end of the Trojan War, the Olympian gods started fighting with each other. Artemis criticized her brother Apollo for refusing to fight the sea god Poseidon after having boasted previously that he could beat him. Apollo remained quiet throughout, saying nothing to his sister, but Hera who overheard Artemis rebuked her, challenging her to do better. Artemis, who as before in the Indian Wars, stood against Hera, found herself being challenged by the queen of the gods.

Hera hit Artemis, sending her bow and arrows flying. Artemis ran away crying, whilst her mother Leto picked up her bow and arrows behind her and went looking for her. Artemis had already run to Zeus and complained to him that Hera hit her.[385]

The other instance of Artemis and Hera together occurred when they were attacked by the Aloadai giants, and Artemis caused the giants to kill each other by turning into a deer and running between them, making them spear each other in their confusion. On that occasion Artemis saved Hera from being attacked, illustrating the fact that not all interaction between the two goddesses was hostile.

---

[384] *Dionysiaca 36.28.*
[385] *Illiad 21.470.*

Artemis & Herakles

The paths of Artemis and Herakles seem to cross frequently in the Greek myths. The third of his twelve labours was to capture the Ceritynean Hind, sister to the four which pulled Artemis' chariot. He managed to wound and catch the hind, but then was met by an angry Artemis and Apollo. Herakles explained the reason for his actions, and Artemis healed the hind and let him go on his way with it.

His sixth labour was to kill and drive off the Stymphalian birds, which he did with a bow and arrow after using bronze clappers made by Hephaestus to scare the birds. There was a temple of Artemis Stymphalia at Stymphalos, which had carvings of the Stymphalian birds in it, suggesting a link to the birds, but there is no record of Artemis being upset by Herakles on this occasion.[386]

Callimachus recounts that when she entered Olympus, Herakles challenged Artemis that she should shoot boars and oxen rather than deer and hares as the latter did no harm.[387] However in the same piece he also mentions the other gods laughing at Herakles for his gluttony, as he had the task of bringing in the game which Artemis had killed.

After Artemis, Apollo and Leto persuaded Zeus to release the Titan god Prometheus from his bondage, Herakles was sent to free and bring Prometheus back.[388]

Artemis & Leto

According to Homer Leto was the daughter of the Titan gods Coeus and Phoebe. Her sister was the star goddess Asteria and as we have already seen, she is the mother of Artemis and her twin brother Apollo.

Artemis and Leto were very close. Immediately upon her birth Artemis helped her mother with the delivery of Apollo, which was a difficult

---

[386] *Pausanias 8.22.7.*
[387] *Callimachus, Hymn 3 to Artemis.*
[388] *Valerius Flaccus, Argonautica 4.60.*

birth unlike her own. In depictions on vases and friezes Artemis and Leto are often shown close to each other.

Artemis was vigorous in defending her mother, and would kill anyone who threatened or impugned her. At Leto's request Artemis killed the daughters of Queen Niobe. With Apollo she killed the giant Tityos who tried to molest Leto. She also killed the Python with Apollo for chasing Leto when she was pregnant, and many rulers for turning the pregnant Leto away.

Leto looked after Artemis like a good mother. When Artemis returned to Olympus, Leto was described as covering Artemis' shoulders, trimming her disordered hair, pulling down her robe and arranging her bow and arrows.[389]

When Artemis fled to Zeus after being hit by Hera, it was Leto who retrieved her bow and arrows which fell to the ground.[390] Leto was also described as having her "heart beat happily" when Artemis and her nymphs gathered to play.[391]

Artemis & Nemesis

Both Artemis and Nemesis were depicted as winged goddesses, and both were virginal and vengeful, showing a certain commonality. Suidas goes so far as to equate Artemis and Nemesis, claiming that the third century BCE writer Demetrios of Skepsis said this,[392] but he was writing in the tenth century CE, many centuries after the worship of the ancient Greek gods had ended.

In the *Dionysiaca*, Artemis asks Nemesis for her aid in punishing the Titan Aura for abusing her. Aura had stroked her breasts and commented on their fullness, saying that her own body was much better, being more muscular.[393] Artemis asked Nemesis to turn Aura into stone, but Nemesis declined, pointing out that she herself was a

---

[389] *Achilleid 1.344.*
[390] *Illiad 21.470.*
[391] *Odyssey 6.102.6.*
[392] *Suidas, Arasteia*
[393] *Dionysiaca 48.351-69.*

Titan. Instead she promised to make Aura lose her highly prized virginity, and made Dionysus fall in love with her and molest her.[394]

Artemis & Pan

The main connection between Artemis and Pan is that he gave her the pack of hunting dogs she used to hunt with, although both are also deities associated with the wilderness.

As with other gods, when Pan tries to molest her nymphs, Artemis does not get angry with him, although on one occasion she was described as complaining when Pan chased her nymphs.[395]

Pausanias refers to a sanctuary of Asclepius at Sikyon, with an image of Pan sitting on one side of the enclosure, and Artemis standing on the other side.[396]

Artemis & Selene

> "Chrysippus in his Old Physics, shows that Artemis is Selene and credits it with an influence on childbirth, says that at the full moon not only do women have the easiest labour but all animals have an easy birth."[397]

Selene as a lunar goddess was frequently identified with Artemis. This occurred in the later period, from around the second century BCE onwards.[398]

> "Both Helios and Selene are closely associated with these [Apollo & Artemis], since they are the causes of the temperature of the air. And both pestilential diseases and

---

[394] *Dionysiaca 48.470-3.*
[395] *Silvae 2.3.1.*
[396] *Pausanias 2.10.2-3.*
[397] *Greek Lyric I Alcaeus Frag 390 (from Scholiast on Illiad).*
[398] See e.g. *Cicero, De Natura Deorum 2.27, 3.19.*

sudden deaths are imputed to these gods [Apollo & Artemis]."[399]

Artemis & Zeus

"It was your wife, Hera of the white arms, who hit me, father, since hatred and fighting have fastened upon the immortals"[400]

Artemis was one of Zeus' favourite children. Callimachus describes the young Artemis sitting on Zeus' knee and making lots of demands for what she wanted, including as many names as Apollo, a bow and arrows, eighty nymphs, all the mountains in the world, and a city. Zeus gave her everything she asked for and more, giving her sixty cities and making her guardian over streets and harbours.[401]

In return, Artemis did not seem to bear any ill will to her father when he seduced her attendant nymphs, as was the case for Callisto, and Taygete. She was also described as weaving Zeus' robes for him, with Athena and Persephone.[402]

---

[399] *Strabo 14.1.6.*
[400] *Illiad 21.470.*
[401] *Callimachus, Hymn 3 to Artemis.*
[402] *Diodorus Siculus 5.2.3.*

17. The Companions of Artemis

Artemis is often shown in the myths as having companions, many of these female. Some of these were mortal and some were deities.

Her companions had almost always taken a vow of chastity, which was sometimes broken through rape, leading to vengeance of one type or another – usually resulting in the death or metamorphosis of the companion.

Being a companion to Artemis had its risks. A number of her companions were seduced or raped by gods. This is something that Artemis was aware of, and made comment on.

> *"Shall I never keep this unseemly, wanton brood from lustful rapine? Must my chaste band of followers ever grow fewer?"*[403]

Artemis had a wide range of companions for company. Foremost of these were the eighty nymphs she requested as a child from Zeus. These were the Amnisiades, twenty nymphs who were daughters of the Cretan river god Amninos, and sixty of the (three thousand) Oceanides, sea nymphs. Other nymphs also joined her retinue as she travelled across the lands.

> *"[Artemis to Zeus] 'And give me sixty daughters of Oceanus (Oceanides) for my choir – all nine years old, all maidens yet ungirdled; and give me for handmaidens twenty Nymphs of Amnisos who shall tend well my buskins, and, when I shoot no more at lynx or stag, shall tend my swift hounds.'"*[404]

Amethyst

Amethyst was a nymph who was transformed into stone by Artemis. Aristotle tells the tale of Amethyst, who was the unfortunate nymph who encountered Dionysus when he was in a bad mood and had

---

[403] *Silvae 2.3.1.*
[404] *Callimachus, Hymn 3 to Artemis.*

sworn to kill the next mortal he met. Amethyst cried out to Artemis, who transformed her into a white piece of stone. Dionysus then felt remorse and poured wine over the stone, turning it purple. From this came the gemstone amethyst, which was though to protect against drunkenness (amethyst means *"not drunk"* or *"against drunkenness"*).

Antikleia

The Phocian princess Antikleia, who married Laertes and became the mother of the hero Odysseus, was another favourite companion of Artemis in her maiden youth.[405] When he visited the underworld, Odysseus first discovered his mother had died, and asked her if Artemis had slain her.[406] Antikleia replies it was not Artemis that killed her, but her longing for the company and counsel of him.

Arethousa

The Arcadian nymph Arethousa was a companion of Artemis before her transformation into the sacred spring at her Syrakousan shrine in Sicily to save her from rape by the river god Alpheios.[407] Pausanias describes a ritual performed at the sanctuary of *Artemis Soteira* at Aegium where offering cakes were taken from the sanctuary and thrown into the sea, with the priests declaring they sent the cakes to Arethousa in Syrakouse.[408] Aelian makes mention of a tame sacred eel at the spring of Arethousa.[409]

Atalanta

The Skhoinean princess Atalanta was abandoned in the wilds at the order of her father King Iasios, who had wanted a son. Artemis took pity on the baby girl and sent a she-bear to raise her. As she grew up

---

[405] *Callimachus, Hymn 3 to Artemis.*
[406] *Odyssey, 11.172.*
[407] *Ovid, Metamorphoses 5.610, Pausanias 5.7.2.*
[408] *Pausanias, 7.24.3.*
[409] *Aelian, On Animals 8.4.*

Artemis taught her the ways of the animals, archery and how to hunt, and she became the fastest runner in Greece and a very good hunter. She forswore love and was a dedicated follower of Artemis for many years.[410]

It was Atalanta, when she was only seventeen, who first wounded the Calydonian Boar, allowing the other hunters to finish it off, despite their protests at her presence on the hunt. Some versions of the myth have the fighting after the death of the boar being started by Meleagros giving the skin to Atalanta for first wounding the boar, and because he was in love with her.[411]

When her father learned of Atalanta's fame, he beseeched her to return to him. Embarassed by his tears, Atalanta agreed to go to the city and learn the ways of civilization. She refused to marry, however, saying she would only marry the man who could outrun her in a race. Any suitor who raced her and lost would be killed.

Aphrodite intervened and gave Hippomenes three golden apples from the garden of the Hesperides. During the race he dropped the apples at different times, which caught Atalanta's eye and she stopped to pick them up. In so doing she lost the race, and Hippomenes gained Atalanta for his wife. Aphrodite, having stolen one of Artemis' maidens, was not content, as the lovers did not thank her. She caused them to have sex in a cave sacred to Cybele, who turned them into lions, and yoked them to her chariot to be her steeds.[412]

Beroe

The goddess Beroe, daughter of Aphrodite and Adonis, hunted with Artemis in her maiden years, carrying the hunting nets.[413] Beroe was wooed by two gods who desired her, Dionysus and Poseidon. She wished to remain maiden, but Zeus intervened and set a contest

---

[410] *Callimachus, Hymn 3 to Artemis.*
[411] *Apollodorus, The Library 1.66.*
[412] *Ovid, Metamorphoses, 10.98.*
[413] *Dionysiaca 41.51.*

between the two gods, which Poseidon won, and thus gained her hand in marriage.[414]

Britomartis

> *"Which of the Nymphs dost thou [Artemis] love above the rest ... Beyond others thou lovest the Nymph of Gortyn, Britomartis, slayer of stags, the goodly archer."*[415]

Britomartis was originally a goddess, but is also described as a Cretan girl who is made immortal after jumping into the sea to escape the lusts of King Minos. She took refuge with some fishermen who hid her in their nets, which some sources claim is why she was also called Diktynna (meaning *she of the nets*).

After this one of the fishermen called Andromedes attempted to molest her, but she fled into a grove on Aigina and disappeared through the intervention of Artemis. As a result of this she was also known as Aphaia (meaning *one who disappeared*), and a temple was set up to her in the grove where she disappeared.

Britomartis presided over the shrines of her tutelary goddess and rescuer Artemis on the islands of Aigina and Crete.[416]

Callisto

The Arcadian princess Callisto was a hunting companion and close friend of Artemis until Zeus raped her. Artemis made Callisto her chief companion until her molestation at the hands of Zeus.

> *"She touched the goddess' bow: 'this bow I touch,' she cried, 'Be a witness to my virginity.' Artemis praised her, and said: 'Keep the pledge you vowed and you will be my companions' princeps.'*[417]

---

[414] *Dionysiaca 41.51f.*
[415] *Callimachus, Hymn 3 to Artemis.*
[416] *Antoninus Liberalis, Metamorphoses 40.*
[417] *Ovid, Fasti 2.155.*

For more on Callisto see the section *Callisto's Fall* in chapter 5 *The Role of Artemis in the Myths*.

Iphigeneia

Iphigeneia was described as a Mycenaean princess, daughter of Agamemnon, who Artemis saved after she was offered as a placatory sacrifice for her father's boasts. Iphigeneia presided over the shrine in Scythian Tauros on the Black Sea. (For more information on Iphigeneia see chapter 8 *Goddess of Women*).

Kyrene

Kyrene, alternatively described as a nymph or a Thessalian princess, was a companion of Artemis until her seduction by Apollo.[418] Kyrene killed a lion with her bare hands, showing her strength and prowess.[419] Kyrene was another beloved companion, whom Artemis gave two hunting dogs before her seduction.[420]

Muses

Although primarily attendants of Apollo, the nine Muses were also occasional companions of Artemis.[421] Artemis also joined them in singing and dancing, two of the activities they inspired most.[422]

---

[418] *Apollonius Rhodius, Argonautica 2.498.*
[419] *Dionysiaca 25.180.*
[420] *Callimachus, Hymn 3 to Artemis.*
[421] *Homeric Hymn 27 to Artemis.*
[422] *Homeric Hymn 3 to Pythian Apollo.*

Nikaia

The Phrygian nymph Nikaia was a companion of Artemis, who killed a besotted shepherd by shooting him with her bow. This incensed Eros, who caused Dionysus to molest her when she was sleeping.[423]

Pholoe

Pholoe, a nymph from central Italy, was a companion of Artemis until she was transformed into a spring to save her from rape at the hands of Pan. Artemis threw an arrow at Pholoe so it struck her left hand and transformed her.[424]

Phylomone

Phylomone, another Arcadian princess, was a hunting companion of Artemis until her seduction by the war god Ares in the guise of a shepherd.[425]

Pleiades

The Pleiades (*doves*) were the seven daughters of the Titan Atlas and the nymph Pleione. They were companions to Artemis for a while, and were nurses and teachers to the young Dionysus. They were pursued by Orion for seven years,[426] and were initially changed into doves and then into stars by Zeus to escape his attentions. It was claimed that was why Orion was close to the constellation of the Pleiades, as even then he still tried to pursue them.[427] Of the seven Pleiades, six of them had sex with gods, and one with a mortal. This was given as the reason why only six of the seven stars in the

---

[423] *Dionysiaca 16.392.*
[424] *Silvae 2.3.1.*
[425] *Plutarch, Greek & Roman Parallel Stories 36.*
[426] *Hyginus, Astronomica 2.21.*
[427] *Pindar, Odes Nemean 2 str 3.*

Pleaides were clearly visible.[428] The eldest of the Pleiades, Maia, was mother of Hermes by Zeus.

Prokris

The Attican lady Prokris hunted with Artemis prior to her marriage to Kephalos. When Kephalos abandoned Prokris for the goddess of the dawn Eos, Artemis helped her regain her husband. She gave Prokris a hunting dog that no prey could escape from, and a javelin that never missed the mark, to give her husband as gifts to tempt him back, a ploy which worked.[429] A later account has Prokris trying to rejoin Artemis and her followers after her husband was unfaithful, but Artemis sent her away as she was no longer a virgin.[430]

Syrinx

Syrinx, an Arcadian nymph, was another companion of Artemis, who was said to look very similar to Artemis.[431] She was transformed into river reeds to save her from rape at the hands of the god Pan, who had been inspired by Aphrodite, angered at Syrinx's chastity.[432] Pan mourning her loss turned her into his pipes to keep her forever close.[433]

---

[428] *Hyginus, Astronomica 2.21.*
[429] *Callimachus, Hymn 3 to Artemis.*
[430] *Hyginus, Fabulae 189.*
[431] *Ovid, Metamorphoses 1.689.*
[432] *Ovid, Metamorphoses 1.689.*
[433] *Dionysiaca 42.363.*

18. Temple Attendants

A number of companions or attendants of Artemis became guardians of specific temples. Bird-legged nymphs were said to attend the Stymphalian shrine of Artemis in Arcadia in southern Greece.[434]

Artemis granted a number of maidens immortality so they could eternally guard her shrines. She granted a girl called Aspalis immortality after she hung herself before her wedding to preserve her virginity, and she became the guardian spirit of Artemis' shrine in Melite in northern Greece.

She also made three Hyperborean maidens called Hekaerge, Loxo and Oupis immortal to be attendants of her shrine on her birth island of Delos. Different sources refer to these maidens, including Callimachus, who declares they were all the daughters of Boreas, the North Wind.[435] They are also mentioned by Nonnus,[436] and Hekaerge and Oupis are mentioned by Pausanias when referring to Delos.[437]

A Spartan princess called Phylonoe (alternatively called Polyboia) was made immortal by Artemis and charged to watch over her Spartan shrines.[438]

Two other princesses called Hemithea and Parthenos, from the island of Naxos, were made immortal by Apollo, to tend the Anatolian shrines of Artemis at Bubastos and Kastabos.

Artemis also sometimes rewarded women who had demonstrated selfless behaviour. A Theban Lady called Makaria-Eukleia, who sacrificed herself to save her family, and died a virgin, was immortalised to look after the shrines of Boiotia in southern Greece.[439]

---

[434] *Pausanias 8.22.4.*
[435] *Callimachus, Hymn 4 to Delos, 292.*
[436] *Dionysiaca 48.302, 48.330 and 5.480.*
[437] *Pausanias 1.43.4, 5.7.8.*
[438] *Pausanias 3.19.4 and Apollodorus 3.126.*
[439] *Plutarch, Aristides 20.5.*

On occasion Artemis also favoured a man with immortality as a shrine attendant. The Troizenoan prince Hippolytus, a companion of Artemis, was slain through the wiles of Aphrodite. The god of healing Asclepius brought Hippolytus back to life, and Artemis made him the attendant of her Arician shrine in Italy.[440] This tale is recounted in great detail by Euripides in his play *Hippolytus*.

---

[440] *Pausanias 2.27.4.*

19. Artemis & Men

As has already been shown, Artemis did have male worshippers and men did attend some of her shrines and temples. The best known of these was Prince Hippolytus of Troizenos, son of Theseus and Queen Hippolytus. He dedicated himself to a chaste life as a hunter, worshipping Artemis and being blessed with her company. He was killed through the wiles of Aphrodite for neglecting her, and Artemis persuaded Asclepius to bring him back to life and made him one of her temple attendants.

In Sparta during the Roman period, young men had to undergo severe flogging until the altar of *Artemis Orthia* was smeared with blood. This ritual flogging was known as *diamastigosis*, and was a test of endurance to demonstrate the worthiness of the young would-be warriors.

The origins of this ceremony were said to come from the discovery of an image of *Artemis Orthia* that was lost from a temple and rediscovered. Two Spartan warriors called Astrabakos and Alopekos found the statue of Artemis and went insane. After a temple was set up around the statue for her, Artemis was temporarily propitiated. However during a sacrifice to her, groups of Limnatians, Kynosourians and Mesoans started quarreling and many were killed at the altar. Artemis in her wrath slew the rest through disease.

When they appealed to an oracle the Spartans were told the only way to appease Artemis was to stain the altar with human blood. Initially they chose lots and give Artemis a human sacrifice, until the whipping of boys seeking to enter manhood was substituted, ensuring a plentiful supply of blood for the altar.[441] The priestess would hold the light wooden image during the scourging, which would grow very heavy if the men scourging gave light blows to a boy because of his beauty or rank. Then the priestess would chastise the scourgers and make sure the boy was scourged appropriately.

---

[441] *Pausanias 3.16.7.*

Another instance where flogging came into play was the archaic cheese-stealing ritual, quoted by Xenophon.[442] Two opposing groups of young men would contest some cheese, stored on the altar. The first group defended the cheese with whips, and the second group tried to steal it.

Euripides refers to a mock sacrifice performed at the temple of *Artemis Tauropolos* in Attica, where a man would have his neck scratched with a knife, so that blood was drawn. It is very tempting to see this as part of an initiatory rite as well, with the first violent blood being shed in honour of Artemis.

> *"And institute this custom: when the people celebrate, as atonement for your sacrifice let them hold a sword to a man's neck and cause blood to flow, for holiness's sake and that the goddess have due honour."*[443]

With the frequent references to Artemis in association with war, and celebrations of battles being dedicated to her, it is clear that Artemis was also honoured by men as well as women, though for different reasons.

---

[442] *Lakedaimonion Politeia 2.9.*
[443] *Euripides, Iphigeneia in Tauris, 1458-61.*

Appendixes

I. The Plants of Artemis

Sacred Plants

Among the plants held sacred to Artemis were amaranth (*amarantos*), cypress (*kyparissos*), palm and walnut (*karya*). Amaranth may have been connected to Artemis via her cult at Amarynthos on the Greek island of Euboia.

Cypress was sacred to Artemis due to her birth occurring in a grove of cypress trees (though other versions of the myth say she was born under a palm tree). For this reason temples and sanctuaries to Artemis were often built within cypress groves.[444]

Alternative versions of her birth have it occurring under a palm tree, which was also sacred to her mother Leto.

> "*The old palm tree [of Delos] played midwife for Leto with her poor little leaves.*"[445]

White poppies were said to be significant in the worship of Artemis in Attica, and a group of bronze statuettes of Artemis from Lousoi in Arcadia (c. 470-400 BCE) show her holding a poppy.[446]

Artemisia

Two herbs renowned for their psychoactive properties are named after Artemis – Mugwort (*Artemisia vulgaris*) and Wormwood (*Artemisia absinthium*). Wormwood is also the herb that is used to make the drink which was favoured by many artists and poets, it was said to induce visions of fairies and as it is a green coloured liquor it was sometimes called the *green fairy*.

---

[444] *Strabo 14.1.20.*
[445] *Dionysiaca 27.259.*
[446] *The Light of the Gods* – Eva Parisinou, p81, p189 n5.

"Of these worts that we name Artemisia, it is said that Diana did find them and delivered their powers and leechdom to Chiron the Centaur, who first from these worts set forth a leechdom, and he named these worts from the name of Diana, Artemis, that is Artemisia."[447]

Gerrard however gives another reason for the name, saying: *"Mugwort is called in Latine, Artemisia, which name it had of Artemisia Queene of Halicarnassus, and wife of noble Mausolus King of Caria, who adopted it for her owne herbe."*[448]

Mugwort is also known as Artemis Herb and Artemisia. A charm for gaining strength to run or for long walks is to pick mugwort before sunrise saying "Tollam te artemesia, ne lassus sum in via." And carry it for the duration of the activity.

---

[447] *Herbarium of Apuleius.*
[448] *Gerrard's Herbal, p254.*

II. Symbols of Artemis

Artemis has a variety of sacred symbols. She is best known for her golden bow and arrows, her chariot drawn by four golden-horned deer, and her sacred animals (discussed earlier).

Artemis' golden bow and arrows could be used not only for killing the animals she hunted, but also to bring disease and sudden death to people. Artemis was also shown at times carrying hunting spears, emphasising her role as huntress.

> "Tired after the hunt, the goddess loved her Nymphs to bathe her with the water's balm ... she gave her spear and quiver and bow unstrung to an attendant Nymph."[449]

Artemis' chariot was golden, and was pulled by four giant golden-horned deer. These deer were captured by Artemis when she was very young, and were the first prey she ever hunted. All of the tracery (reins, yokes, etc) of her chariot were also golden.[450]

Like her brother Apollo, Artemis was also associated with music, and was frequently depicted carrying a lyre. There are a number of references to her in connection with dance (see chapter 10 *Goddess of the Dance & Song*).

A poem by Antipater combined several of the symbols of Artemis in her honour:

> "Sosis, Phila and Polycrates dedicate this harp, this bow and these intricate nets. The archer dedicates his bow of horn, the musician her tortoise-shell lyre and the hunter his woven nets. Let the first win prize for archery, the next for harp-playing and the third in the hunting world."[451]

Artemis was often represented bearing a torch. This was a common representation for Greek goddesses, but there are several

---

[449] *Metamorphoses 3.138.*
[450] *Callimachus, Hymn 3 to Artemis.*
[451] *Antipater, The Offering of the Winners.*

distinguishing features in her case. The torches may have had a variety of uses. These include use for combat, illumination of night ceremonies or hunting, and purification.

> *"She [Artemis] will forsake your miseries and will dissolve the deadly pharmaka of pestilence by melting down with her flame-bearing torches, in nightly fire, the kneaded wax figurines, the evil signs of the magos' art."*[452]

Along with Hekate, Artemis is often shown bearing two torches. Unlike Hekate, Artemis was shown bearing two long torches, rather than the two short torches of Hekate.[453] These images start occurring from the middle of the 5th century BCE, and usually show Artemis receiving worshippers or sacrifices.

A late 5th century BCE cup by Aristophanes shows Artemis with her two torches fighting a Titan, accompanied by Zeus with his thunderbolt fighting another Titan.[454] This theme of Artemis with two torches fighting giants is also seen on a late 5th century BCE plate at the British Museum.[455]

Three late 4th or early 3rd century BCE votive reliefs from Ekhinos and Delos to Artemis Lokhia, possibly representing thanks for successful births, all show Artemis with a long torch.

Euripides describes Iphigeneia using torchlight to purify the statue of Artemis from the matricides committed in its presence.[456]

A custom which was re-instituted for the modern Olympic Games is that of the torch race. In ancient Greece, torch races, where the winner would light the sacrificial flame with his torch, were practiced in honour of several deities. The best known of these is the goddess Athena, but this also seems to have been the case for *Artemis*

---

[452] *Oracle of Ephesus*, quoted in *Magic, Religion, and Syncretism at the Oracle of Claros* – Z. Várhelyi p16, in *Between Magic and Religion*, 2001.
[453] See Athens National Museum 1950, 1892; 2376, 2445 Athens Akropolis Museum 2674; Brauron Archaeological Museum 1182(1).
[454] Staatliche Museum, Berlin, F2531, cat no 7.18.
[455] British Museum E701, London.
[456] *Euripides, Iphigeneia in Tauris, 2:1224-5.*

Tauropolos.[457] Torch-bearing girls are also seen in depictions from the temple of Artemis at Brauron.

A special series of cult vessels called *krateriskoi* have been excavated at Brauron. These were used for dedications to Artemis. They depict naked girls running, as well as part of a bear, all perhaps pictorial renderings of the Brauronian rituals. A pit containing small votive offerings and geometric potsherds has also been unearthed.

[457] *The Light of the Gods* – Eva Parisinou, p38.

III. An Artemis Curse

A good example of a curse involving Artemis from the 6th century BCE gives her acting in conjunction with her brother Apollo, their mother Leto and the goddess of wisdom Athena. This curse is actually part of an oath, called the Amphictyonic oath, and referred to an obligation not to till the sacred plain of Cirrha.

> *"Let them be under the curse of Apollo and Artemis and Leto and Athena Pronaea. The curse goes on: that their land bear no fruit that their wives bear children not like those who begat them, but monsters; that their flocks yield not their natural increase; that defeat awaits them in camp and court and market place; and that they perish utterly, themselves, their houses, their whole race. And never may they offer pure sacrifice unto Apollo, nor to Artemis, nor to Leto, nor to Athena Pronaea, and may the gods refuse their offerings."[458]*

---

[458] *The Speeches of Aeschines, Aeshin, Or. 3.111; translation by Ch.D. Adams.*

IV. Dateline for Source Material

— Homer - 9th-8th century BCE
— Hesiod - 8th-7th century BCE
— The Homeric Hymns - 8th-4th century BCE
— Alkman – 7th century BCE
— Greek Lyric Fragments - 7th-6th century BCE
— Etymologicum Magnum – 7th-6th century BCE
— Hipponax – 6th century BCE
— Aiskhylos – 6th-5th century BCE
— Euripides – 5th century BCE
— Herodotus - 5th century BCE
— Pindar - 5th century BCE
— Sophocles – 5th century BCE
— Aristophanes - 5th-4th century BCE
— Plato – 5th-4th century BCE
— Xenophon – 5th-4th century BCE
— The Orphic Hymns - uncertain century BCE
— Antipater – 4th century BCE
— Theocritus – 4th-3rd century BCE
— Callimachus – 3rd century BCE
— Apollonius Rhodius - 3rd century BCE
— Apollodorus - 2nd century BCE
— Servius Sulpicius Rufus – 2nd century BCE
— Cicero – 1st century BCE
— Diodorus Siculus - 1st century BCE
— Virgil - 1st century BCE
— Homerica, The Contest of Homer & Hesiod, Aethiopica, Cypria - BCE
— Ovid - 1st century BCE - 1st century CE
— Strabo - 1st century BCE - 1st century CE
— Pliny the Elder - 1st century CE
— Statius - 1st century CE
— Valerius Flaccus – 1st century CE
— Plutarch - 1st-2nd century CE
— Ptolemy Hephaestion - 1st-2nd century CE
— Antoninus Liberalis – 2nd century CE
— Apuleius – 2nd century CE

— Hyginus - 2nd century CE
— Pausanias - 2nd century CE
— Philostratus - 2nd century CE
— Aelian - 2nd-3rd century CE
— Cassius Dio – 2nd-3rd century CE
— Oppian – 2nd-3rd century CE
— Athenaios – 3rd century CE
— Lactantius – 3rd-4th century CE
— Porphyry – 3rd-4th century CE
— Quintus Smyrnaeus - 4th century CE
— Nonnus - 5th century CE
— Proclus – 5th century CE
— Colluthus - 5th-6th century CE
— Suidas - 10th century CE

Bibliography

Aelian, *On the Characteristics of Animals Books I-V*, 1958, Harvard University Press, Harvard
---------- *On the Characteristics of Animals Books VI-X*, 1958, Harvard University Press, Harvard
---------- *On the Characteristics of Animals Books XII-XVII*, 1958, Harvard University Press, Harvard
Apuleius , *The Golden Ass*, 1990, Harvard University Press, Harvard
Asirvatham, S, & Pache, C.O (eds), *Between Magic and Religion 2001*, Rowman & Littlefield Publishers Inc, Oxford
Athanassakis, A. (trans), *Hesiod: Theogony, Works and Days, Shield*, 1984, John Hopkins University Press, Baltimore
---------- *The Orphic Hymns: Text, Translation and Notes*, 1988, Society of Biblical Literature, Atlanta
Austin, Colin (ed), *Aristophanes Thesmophoriazusae*, 2004, Oxford University Press, Oxford
Avagianou, Aphrodite, *Sacred Marriage in the Rituals of Greek Religion*, 1991, Peter Lang, Bern
Baugh, S.M. *Cult Prostitution in New Testament Ephesus: A Reappraisal*, 1999 in Journal of the Evangelical Theological Society, 42.3, 443-60
Betz, Hans Dieter (ed), *The Greek Magical Papyri in Translation*, 1986, University of Chicago Press, Chicago
Boardman, John, *Athenian Black Figure Vases*, 1974, Thames & Hudson, London
---------- *Greek Sculpture: The Archaic Period*, 1978, Thames & Hudson, London
Bonner, C., *Studies in Magical Amulets, Chiefly Graeco-Egyptian*, 1950, Ann Arbor, Michigan
Brewster, Harry, *The River Gods of Greece*, 1997, I.B. Tauris & Co. Ltd, London
Burkert, W., *Greek Religion*, 1987, Harvard University Press, Harvard
Calame, Claude, *Choruses of Young Women in Ancient Greece: Their Morphology, Religious Role, and Social Functions*, 1997, Rowman & Littlefield Publishers Inc, Maryland
Callimachus, *Hymns, Epigrams, Select Fragments*, 1988, John Hopkins University Press, Baltimore
Campbell, D.A., *Greek Lyric: Sappho Alcaeus*, 1982, Harvard University Press, Harvard
---------- *Greek Lyric III: Stesichorus, Ibycus, Simonides and Others*, 1991, Harvard University Press, Harvard
---------- *Greek Lyric V: The New School of Poetry and Anonymous Songs and Hymns*, 1993, Harvard University Press, Harvard
Carpenter, Rhys, *Folk Tale, Fiction and Saga in the Homeric Epics*, 1946, University of California Press, Los Angeles
Carter, Jane Burr, *The Masks of Ortheia*, 1987, in American Journal of Archaeology 91.3:355-384
Cicero, *De Natura Deorum*, 2003, Cambridge University Press, Cambridge
Clauss, James J. & Johnston, Sarah Iles, *Medea*, 1997, Princeton University Press, Princeton
Clement, Paul, *New Evidence for the Origin of the Iphigeneia Legend*, 1934, in L'Antiquité Classique 3:393-409

Clinton, Kevin, *Artemis and the Sacrifice of Iphigeneia in Aeschylus' Agamemnon*, 1988, in *Language and the Tragic Hero*, Scholars Press, USA

Colluthus, *The Rape of Helen*, 1993, Königshausen & Neumann, Germany

Condos, Theony (trans), *Star Myths of the Greeks and Romans: A Sourcebook, Containing the Constellations of Pseudo-Erastophenes and the Poetic Astronomy of Hyginus*, 1997, Phanes Press, Minnesota

Cook, Arthur Bernard, *Zeus: A Study in Ancient Religion (3 volumes)*, 1914, Cambridge University Press, Cambridge

Deubner, Ludwig, *Attische Feste*, 1932, Berlin

Dietrich, B.C., *The Origins of Greek Religion*, 1974, Walter De Gruyter, Berlin

Dowden, Ken, *Death and the Maiden: Girls' Initiation Rites in Greek Mythology*, 1989, Routledge, London

Fagles, Robert (trans), *The Odyssey*, 1999, Penguin Books, London

Faraone, Christopher, & Obbink, Dirk (eds), *Magika Hiera: Ancient Greek Magic & Religion*, 1991, Oxford University Press, Oxford

Farnell, Lewis R., *The Cults of the Greek States (5 volumes)*, 1896, Clarendon Press, Oxford

Fauth, W., *Arktos in den griechischen Zauberpapyri*, 1984, in *Zeitschrift fur Papyrologie und Epigraphik 57*

Fitzgerald, Robert (trans), *The Aeneid (Virgil)*, 1990, Vintage, Canada

Flaccus, *Voyage of the Argo: The Argonautica of Gaius, Valerius Flaccus*, 1999, John Hopkins University Press, Baltimore

Ford, Andrew, *The Origins of Criticism: Literary Culture and Poetic Theory in Classical Greece*, 2002, Princeton University Press, Princeton

Frazer, J.G. (trans), *Apollodorus: The Library*, 1960, Harvard University Press, Harvard

Gager, John G., *Curse Tablets and Binding Spells from the Ancient World*, 1992, Oxford University Press, Oxford

Garrison, Daniel H., *Sexual Culture in Ancient Greece*, 2000, Univeristy of Oklahoma Press, Oklahoma

Gershenson, Daniel, *Apollo the Wolf God*, 1991, Institute for the Study of Man, Virginia

Gordon, R.L., *Myth, religion and society*, 1977, Cambridge University Press, Cambridge

Graf, Fritz, *Magic in the Ancient World*, 1997, Harvard University Press, Massachusetts

Green, Peter (trans), *The Argonautika (Apollonius Rhodius)*, 1997, University of California Press, California

Habicht, Christian, *Pausanias' Guide to Greece*, 1998, University of California Press, California

Herodotus, *The Histories*, 1992, W.W. Norton & Co, New York

Hesiod, *The Homeric Hymns and Homerica*, 1981, Harvard University Press, Harvard

Hopfner, T., *Hekate-Selene-Artemis und Verwandte in den griechischen Zauberpapyri und auf den Fluchtafeln, Piscicul, Festschrift F.J.Dolger*

Hughes, Dennis D., *Human Sacrifice in Ancient Greece*, 1991, Routledge, London

Hull, D.B., *Hounds and Hunting in Ancient Greece*, 1964, University of Chicago Press, Chicago

Johnson, Buffie, *Lady of the Beasts*, 1994, Inner Traditions International, Vermont

Johnston, Sarah Iles, *Hekate Soteira*, 1990, Scholars Press, Georgia

Kahil, L., *Autour de l'Artemis Attique*, 1965, in *Antike Kunst 8:20-33*

---------- *L'Artemis de Brauron: rites et mystere*, 1977, in *Antike Kunst 20:86-98*

---------- *Artemis*, 1984, in *Lexicon iconographicum mythologiae classicae 2:618-753*

Kassel, R., & Austin, C., *Poetae Comici Graeci*, 1983, Walter De Gruyter Inc, New York

Kerényi, C., *Zeus and Hera*, 1975, Routledge & Kegan Paul, London

---------- *The Gods of the Greeks*, 1951, Thames & Hudson, London

Larson, Jennifer, Greek Heroine Cults, 1995, University of Wisconsin Press, Madison

Lattimore, Richard (trans), The Illiad of Homer, 1961, University of Chicago Press, Chicago

----------- (trans), The Odes of Pindar, 1976, University of Chicago Press, Chicago

----------- (trans), Four Plays by Aristophanes: The Birds, The Clouds, The Frogs, Lysistrata, 1984, Plume, USA

----------- (trans), Iphigeneia in Taurus (Euripides), 1992, Oxford University Press, Oxford

Leslie, Shane, The Greek Anthology, 1929, Ernest Benn Ltd, London

Letharby, W.R., The Earlier Temple of Artemis at Ephesus, 1917, Journal of Hellenic Studies, 37:1-16

Liberalis Antoninus, Metamorphoses, 1992, Routledge, London

Lloyd-Jones, P.H.J., Artemis and Iphigeneia, 1983, in The Journal of Hellenic Studies 103:87-102

Lombardo, S. (trans), Callimachus: Hymns, Epigrams, Select Fragments, 1988, John Hopkins University Press, Baltimore

Lonsdale, Steven H., Dance and Ritual Play in Greek Religion, 1993, John Hopkins University Press, Baltimore

Luck, George, Arcana Mundi: Magic and the Occult in the Greek and Roman Worlds, 1995, John Hopkins University Press, Baltimore

Marinatos, Nannó, The Goddess and the Warrior: The Naked Goddess and Mistress of Animals in Early Greek Religion, 2000, Routledge, London

Marshall, Peter, Hyginus: Fabulae, 2002, K.G. Saur Verlag, Germany

Masson, O., Les fragments du poète Hiponnax, 1962, Paris

Moon, Warren G., Ancient Greek Art and Iconography, 1983, University of Wisconsin Press, Wisconsin

Murphy, Trevor (trans), Pliny the Elder's Natural History, 2004, Oxford University Press, Oxford

Nilsson, Martin P., The Minoan-Mycenaean Religion and its Survival in Greek Religion, 1927, Humphrey Milford, London

----------- Homer and Mycenae, 1933, Methuen & Co Ltd, London

Nonnos, Dionysiaca Books I-XV, 1965, Harvard University Press, Harvard

----------- Dionysiaca Books XVI-XXXV, 1965, Harvard University Press, Harvard

----------- Dionysiaca Books XXXVI-XLVIII, 1966, Harvard University Press, Harvard

Oppian, Cynergetica

Ovid, Metamorphoses, 1998, Oxford University Press, Oxford

----------- Fasti, 2000, Penguin Books, London

Parisinou, Eva, The Light of the Gods: The Role of Light in Archaic and Classical Greek Cult, 2000, Gerald Duckworth & Co Lotd, London

Parke, H.W., Festivals of the Athenians, 1977, London

Perlman, Paula, Acting the She-Bear for Artemis, 1989, in Arethusa Vol 22 no.2.

Philostratus, The Life of Apollonius of Tyana, 1912, Harvard University Press, Harvard

Pindar, The Odes and Selected Fragments, 1998, Everyman, London

Plutarch, Lives (2 volumes), 2001, Modern Library, London

----------- Moralia: Roman Questions, Greek Questions, Greek and Roman Parallel Stories, 1936, Harvard University Press, Harvard

Price, T.H., Kourotrophos: Cults and Representations of the Greek Nursing Deities, 1978, E.J. Brill, Leiden

Quintus Smyrnaeus, The Fall of Troy, 1962, Harvard University Press

Rehm, Rush, Marriage to Death: The Conflation of Wedding and Funeral Rituals in Greek Tragedy, 1994, Princeton University Press, New Jersey

Rouse, W.H.D., Nonnus Dionysiaca Books 1-48 (3 volumes), 1960, Harvard University Press, Cambridge

Harvard, von Rudloff, Robert, Hekate in Ancient Greek Religion, 1999, Horned Owl Publishing, Victoria

Sale, William, The Temple Legends of Arkteia, 1975, in Rheinisches Museum für Philologie Volume 1:265-84.

Schefold, Karl, Myth and Legend in Early Greek Art, 1966, Thames & Hudson, London

Scheid, John, The Craft of Zeus: Myths of Weaving Harvard University Press, Massachusetts

Seltman, Charles, Greek Coins, 1933, Methuen & Co. Ltd, London

Siculus Diodorus, Books I-II, 1985, Harvard University Press, Harvard

---------- Books IV-VIII, 1939, Harvard University Press, Harvard

---------- Books IX-XII, 1939, Harvard University Press, Harvard

---------- Books XVIII-XIX, 1947, Harvard University Press, Harvard

Siebourg, M., Zu den Ephesia Grammata, 1915, in Archiv fur Papyrusforschung 18:594

Simon, Erica, Festivals of Attica, 1983, University of Wisconsin Press, Wisconsin

Simpson, Michael (trans), Gods and Heroes of the Greeks: The Library of Apollodorus, 1976, University of Massachusetts Press, Amherst

Statius, The Thebaid: Seven Against Thebes, 2004, John Hopkins University Press, Baltimore

---------- Silvae, 2003, Harvard University Press, Harvard

---------- Achilleid, 2005, Bristol Phoenix Press, Bristol

Strabo, The Geography of Strabo, 1967, Harvard University Press, Harvard

Swinburne, Algernon Charles, Swinburne's Collected Poetical Works (2 volumes), 1924, William Heinemann, London

Theognis, Elegies of Theognis: A Revised Text Based on a New Collation of the Mutininensis MS, 1979, Ayer Co Publishers, New Hampshire

Thomson, G., The Greek Calendar, 1943, Journal of Hellenic Studies, 63:52-65

Vernant, Jean-Pierre, Myth & Society in Ancient Greece, 1980, Harvester Press Ltd, Brighton

West, M.L., The Hesiodic Catalogue of Women, 1985, Clarendon Press, Oxford

Whalley, Joyce (trans), Pliny the Elder, Historia Naturalis, 1982, Victoria & Albert Museum, London

Willetts, R.F., Cretan Cults and Festivals, 1962, Routledge & Kegan Paul Ltd, London

Xenophon, Die Verfassung Der Spartaner. Lakedaimonion Politeia, 1998, Wissenschaftliche Buchgesellschaft, Hesse

Yavis, C.G., Greek Altars: Origins and Typology, 1949, Saint Louis University Press, Missouri

Websites

Perseus Digital Library Project. Ed. Gregory R. Crane,Tufts University. January 2005, <http://www.perseus.tufts.edu>.

Theoi Project. Ed. Aaron Atsma, January 2005, <http://www.theoi.com>

Index

Atlas, 121
Attic Calendar, 28
Attica, 14, 18, 31, 53, 71, 126, 128
Aulis, 26, 84
Aura, 13, 65, 106, 109, 113
Aureliopos, 81
Azanian Hills, 26, 51
Bargylia, 27, 50
Bastet, 103, 106, 107
Bear, 32, 38, 71, 72, 110, 118, 132
Bees, 13
Bendis, 103, 107
Beroe, 118
Blood, 125, 126
Blood-Price, 71
Boar, 23, 32, 68, 71, 74, 75, 78, 93, 104, 112
Boedromion, 28, 29
Boiai, 26, 56, 78
Boiotia, 123
Boreas, 15, 59, 123
Bosporus Strait, 54
Boubastis, 106
Boulis, 26
Bouphagos, 93
Bouphonion, 28
Bouto, 106
Bow, 8, 13, 36, 43, 61, 68, 69, 83, 85, 86, 90, 97, 101, 111, 112, 113, 115, 119, 121, 130
Brauron, 17, 18, 19, 20, 21, 26, 28, 37, 57, 71, 85, 86, 110, 131, 132
Brauronia, 19, 28
Breasts, 11, 13
Britomartis, 52, 103, 108, 119
Bromia, 58, 109
Bromios, 58, 109

Broteas, 69
Bubastos, 27, 123
Bull, 37, 69, 75, 76
Buzzard, 71, 74
Byzantion, 27, 54
Caino, 108
Cakes, 30
Calendar, 28
Callimachus, 39, 47, 50, 51, 54, 58, 59, 60, 61, 62, 65, 68, 76, 77, 83, 85, 86, 88, 90, 91, 92, 93, 97, 98, 99, 100, 101, 104, 108, 112, 115, 116, 117, 118, 119, 120, 122, 123, 130, 134
Callisto, 38, 97, 115, 119
Calydon, 26, 52, 74
Calydonian Boar, 74, 118
Capua, 27
Carme, 108
Caryatid, 49
Cassius Dio, 57
Cat, 103, 107
Catalogues of Women, 37
Cave, 18
Cedar, 49
Ceritynean Hind, 76, 112
Chalcis, 84
Chariot, 31, 76, 81, 106, 112, 130
Charisteria, 28, 29, 105
Cheese-Stealing Ritual, 126
Chersiphon, 22
Chiron, 129
Chiton, 19
Choregos, 83, 84
Chrestomathia, 67
Chrysippus, 114
Cicero, 114, 134
Cirrha, 133
Clothes, 19, 66, 67

Keres, 91
Khersonesos, 27
Khitone, 59, 68
Khloris, 39
Khronios, 47, 93
Kilikia, 55
Kindye, 50
King Croesus, 22
King Dion, 109
King Kodors, 23
King Lygdamis, 38, 39
King Minos, 108, 119
King Oineus, 74
King Pelias, 35
King Tantalus, 39
King Xerxes, 19, 22
KingTantalos, 69
Kirrha, 26
Kithaironian Lion, 43
Kleanthes, 44
Knageus, 50
Komana, 57
Korakios, 27
Kordax. *See* Cordax
Korone, 26, 60
Koronis, 94
Korythaleia, 52
Kos, 50
Kouretes, 75
Kourotrophos, 52, 59, 66
Krateriskoi, 132
Krokotoi, 20
Kronos, 44
Kynosoura, 49
Kynosourian Bitches, 77
Kyrene, 120
Kyrtones, 26
Lacedaimonia, 29, 45, 48, 49,
  56, 58, 85, 86, 89
Laconia, 109
Lactantius, 42

Ladomeia, 96
Lady of the Beasts, 11
Laertes, 117
Lake Gygaia, 27, 51
Lake Koloe, 51
Lakedaimonion Politeia, 126,
  134
Laphria, 28, 31, 52
Laphros, 52
Lato, 65
Latona, 41, 74, *See* Leo
Leimon, 94
Lenaion, 28
Leopard, 11, 79, 81, 101
Leros, 60
Lesbos, 43
Leto, 3, 10, 14, 15, 16, 34, 39,
  40, 41, 53, 60, 61, 62, 65,
  72, 74, 81, 82, 94, 95, 96,
  103, 104, 108, 110, 111,
  112, 113, 128, 133
Letrinoi, 26, 43
Life of Apollonius of Tyana, 54,
  56, 135
Life of Thesus, 31
Lilaia, 26
Limenoskope, 60
Limnai, 26
Limnaion, 19
Lingerie, 66
Lion, 11, 46, 71, 79, 101, 118
Lítois, 60
Lives, 48, 90
Lomaitho, 58, 94
Lousa, 47
Lousoi, 26, 128
Loxo, 35, 123
Lunar Crescent, 76
Lustration, 20
Lycaon, 38
Lydia, 51, 54, 81, 85

About the Author

Sorita D'Este is a writer and researcher who lives and works in London, UK. She has a passion for the mysteries and gods of the western world and much of her work is focused on the spritiual and magical practices of ancient Greece, Rome and Britian.

She is the co-author of *The Guises of the Morrigan* and *Circle of Fire*. Additionally she is a regular contributor to magazines, part works and journals, including *DeAgostini's Enhancing your Mind Body & Spirit* and *Llewellyn's Annuals.*

For those interested in exploring the mysteries, myths and symbolism of ancient spiritual systems, Sorita facilitates workshops and courses in the UK. She also gives lectures on a variety of related topics at conferences, festivals and seminars in and around Europe.

In addition to her research and writing, she likes spending her time wandering around local woodlands, cycling and dancing.

If you would like to find out more about her work, or have comments on this book that you would like to share, please write to:

Sorita D'Este
C/O BM Avalonia
London
WC1N 3XX
England

CPSIA information can be obtained
at www.ICGtesting.com
Printed in the USA
BVHW071725260521
608083BV00003B/116

9 781905 297023